C000056743

Free Yourself from Emotional Dependence

The 5 steps to finally get out of bonds and addictions that do not make you live the life you deserve

Amanda Reck

Index

Does emotional dependence only occur with violent, narcissistic, or psychopathic people?

Second step - How to end the relationship with a violent manipulator and how to defend yourself in case of need Third step - Practical exercises of self-esteem (the grid of well-being and affirmative rights)

Clues of low self-esteem Affirmative rights

The three moments of the couple

The grid of well-being

Step 4 - Practical exercises to accept, manage and communicate your emotions

Anger Resentment Forgiveness Anxiety

Sadness Jealousy

Envy

Fifth step - The effective way of communication to express needs, necessities, to mediate and defend against the bullying of others

The techniques of effective communication

Conclusions

Introduction

We live in an age of uncertainty, of sudden social and personal changes, of the "liquid" society because it is constantly becoming. We are constantly faced with new situations that we have not been educated to manage because we are used to certainties or control of our lives with the classic phrases: "be content with what you have", "don't leave the old road for the new one", "you know what you leave but not what you find".

We therefore find ourselves in conflict between two opposing tendencies: the need for security, which pushes us to seek control of situations, and the continuous change that society imposes on us.

Added to this are the old rules of relationship based on mutual tolerance, loyalty, staying together for children, parents, home, money but also the fear of getting back into the game or being alone or the social drive to personal well-being, healthy selfishness, freedom, wanting to be happier.

Ours is a schizophrenic reality, because two opposing cultures coexist - the past and the present - that we have not been used to facing, not having the tools to do so.

It is no coincidence that addictions rage: from shopping, alcohol, drugs, work, sex, gambling and not least from affection.

Instead of anesthetizing oneself with all this, one should learn to face pain, to go through it with courage. But to keep up with what society imposes on us (beauty, youth, happiness, competence, success...), more and more people are burying their heads in the sand instead of reflecting on themselves and their lives.

Affective dependence has two protagonists: the dominated and the dominant who, paradoxically, are both chained in the game of violence and manipulation.

Both have suffered in their childhood, but as adults, despite having the same matrix, they develop opposite ways.

Let us explain what happens.

The child needs affection, gratification, attention, support in difficulties and security. If the parent does not meet his needs because he is in difficulty, not serene in his relationship, unhappy or otherwise unsuitable for his role, the child, not being able to make a proper analysis of the situation and considering his dependence on parental figures, if his needs are not met, he blames himself. So, he thinks he is not worth it. He also feels anger, which is also pain, and he feels guilty about it, because for him parents are like gods on which he depends to live.

Little by little his basic beliefs of "worthlessness and guilt" are grafted into the unconscious part, in the right hemisphere of the brain, conditioning his adolescence and his life in three ways.

The first is that of the victim who, feeling inadequate and guilty, will choose partners that will confirm your beliefs, so you may become dependent on relationships.

The second is that of avoidance for which, in order not to be disapproved or feel guilty, the person will try to devote himself to work and others in the hope of avoiding the feeling of inadequacy and guilt, as well as feeling loved.

The third is the mode used by the executioners: convinced that they are not worthy, they need to dominate others, to possess them, to control them, to have power over them for fear of being abandoned and rejected.

Becoming aware of these dynamics is the first step to free themselves from the chains of dependence, in which, I repeat, both sides are trapped.

How to read this book

The first part describes the aspects of addiction, its protagonists and the dynamics that chain them in a spiral of suffering and dissatisfaction. This leads to awareness and acceptance of reality without judgments and guilt.

The second part explains how to get out of prison, with theoretical but above all practical explanations, to provide readers with the tools to take charge of their lives and create satisfying relationships, first and foremost with themselves.

Ultimately, we all deserve to be happy.

First part

Definition of emotional dependence

Chapter 1

Let's define what is emotional dependence

Before we talk about emotional dependence it is necessary to first dwell on the definition of dependence. The term is often used in common language to identify the category of people who use and abuse drugs, sometimes ignoring the fact that there are various forms of addiction not necessarily related to the use of drugs, psychotropic substances, or alcohol.

Addiction can be defined as an alteration in a person's behavior, characterized by intense and often uncontrollable needs towards substances, objects, situations or even other people. This alteration of behavior stems from a habitual search for physical and/or psychological pleasure that over time makes the individual lose control of the situation, leading to a more serious condition, definable pathology.

The addiction can be physical and/or psychic. In physical dependence we see physiological changes in the body of the person and in the functioning of the brain system: drugs, for example, can induce the major and most serious physiological changes, both in the abuse and abstinence phases. Heroin, cocaine, ecstasy, alcohol, and derivatives are (both in the collective imagination and in the clinic) the substances that more than others can lead to particularly serious physical and behavioral consequences.

However, there are also substances that seem to induce minor physical effects. For example, in modern society it is now established that a good slice of the population smokes cigarettes; however, being the "smoker" culturally accepted, there is an almost automatic tendency to underestimate the power of modification in the body that nicotine and the thousands of substances contained with it in cigarette tobacco. In this case the short-term negative effects can be relatively mild but, in the long term, scientific research has shown us that a smoker is more likely than a person who does not smoke to incur in cancer or heart and lung problems even of serious magnitude. There are therefore dependencies on "objects" that only apparently seem to create fewer negative consequences.

If the physical dependence can be overcome with relative ease (there are agonist drugs that progressively reduce the withdrawal symptoms by decreasing the desire to use the substance habitually used), the case of psychic dependence is different: the same acts in fact in an incisive and pervasive way on the way of thinking of the person and consequently on his behavior. If the distinction between physical and psychic dependence can be made on a clinical level, the two forms interact very closely with each other,

creating in fact a situation of high complexity in the treatment and therapeutic rehabilitation of those suffering from this pathology.

Even situations or conditions that do not necessarily have to do with substances can induce physiological changes in the body: think, for example, of gambling, internet addiction, sexual or work addiction, conditions that involve, although at a lower and different level, physiological changes induced by a new way of thinking.

All these forms of addiction have some common aspects, beyond the fact that the object of the problem is a substance, a situation, a person:

- We have the presence of a withdrawal syndrome (otherwise called withdrawal crisis) and that is a serious condition that manifests itself when the use of what causes addiction is suspended. The person, when he stops using the substance or leaves the object of addiction, after a few hours or a few days can become sleepless, have feelings of nausea or vomiting (these feelings can then materialize in actual episodes of vomiting), hallucinate (especially after the use of substances or alcohol), anxiety, difficulty sleeping at night, tremors. All these conditions usually create high stress, such as to affect negatively and significantly in the working, social, relational area.

- We then have a condition of tolerance or habituation: the person feels the need to progressively increase the "dose" (substance or situation that is) to achieve the same effect as previously experienced.

- We have a continuous search for substances (situation or person), which manifests itself with craving, a modification of thought on an impulsive basis that directs the individual only towards the object of desire.

- We are witnessing a more and more serious compromise of the most significant life contexts, such as work, family, social / family. The person puts into action behaviors that are aimed at keeping the addiction alive at the expense of relationships, even the most significant ones, going to meet a relational void and particularly disabling conditions of loneliness.

But what distinguishes emotional dependence from other forms of dependence? Answer: the object of desire, which in this case is represented by a person in the flesh, the partner of our love relationship, the boyfriend, partner, husband, or wife.

Affective dependence

Affective dependence occurs when the affection, attraction, love that we feel towards a person takes on the characteristics of a real addiction, with all the negative particularities that we have seen previously.

All of us have experienced a condition of "healthy" emotional dependence: think, for example, when we were children and were cared for by our parents in an affectionate and balanced way. In this case we have experienced a necessary and useful form of it for the development of our psychophysical well-being and for our growth. During adolescence then most people develop a "healthy" dependence on the peer group, which becomes a point of reference and comparison and helps in the transition from the sometimes-stormy adolescent period to that of adulthood, with all its strengths and weaknesses. Even in the relationship with partners there is a certain degree of dependence: when this allows everyone to feel free to "do and be" within the relationship, then we are talking about a condition of balance where both members benefit from the positive aspects of being together and at the same time face in a mature way any difficulties or differences that naturally exist in the relationship with the other.

When does dependence on the other become a problem?

It becomes so when the partner represents our only goal in life, when we think that he or she can be the one who will solve our personal problems, when we see in the other our absolute ideal of love without having a more realistic vision of it (with pros and cons... and often the latter are very evident but denied, as if we had slices of salami on our eyes!), when our very existence is put in second place to that of our partner.

But then what are the characteristics that distinguish emotional dependence?

First, it must be specified that, contrary to other forms of addiction (drugs, alcohol, cannabis ...), emotional dependence is not currently included among the diseases included in the most widespread diagnostic systems such as DSM-V. The topic was highlighted in the 1970s by Robin Norwood, an American psychologist and family therapist who worked in the field of drug addiction and who wrote the famous book Women Who Love Too Much. In more recent times, even on the wave of a greater popular diffusion of the most popular psychological topics, emotional addiction has become a problem treated more widely, described more clearly and simply, reaching through the media (radio, television, internet) a large part of the population.

Affective dependence is characterized by being persistent; it is therefore a condition that lasts over time, in which the protagonists of the dance of dependence bind each other in a contrasted, ambiguous, at times almost sadistic-masochistic relationship. This persistence lasts for many years: there are couples who will never even become aware of the problem, others who, despite being aware of it, continue to remain in the condition of an uncomfortable love.

It is a condition permeated by obsessiveness (referring both to thoughts and behaviors): both members of the couple can, each in their own way, develop recurring thoughts and similar in content that occupy most of their day. It is even more true for the one who is dominated in the couple, is dependent on the other, since the partner becomes the only and magnificent point of reference in daily life, the sole purpose of the person's life, the object of their "love".

Another characteristic that we can find in the emotional dependent is impulsiveness, that condition that makes us lose the ability to reflect and sometimes pushes us to act instinctively, leading us to say words or perform acts with excessive "spontaneity". In fact, if in some cases an impulsive action can encourage decision making when faced with the resolution of a problem, in most cases such an attitude tends to drive away people around us, creating scorched ground. This happens because the unpredictability of impulsive behavior usually generates a lot of anxiety related to the thought "who knows what will happen".

Next to impulsiveness and even more to obsessive thoughts we can often find compulsive behavior. They are those that are repeated with increasing frequency, from which the person is not able to escape because the will is almost cancelled. Who puts in action these behaviors come reassured from the same ones but, if they are not treated, they consolidate a dependence not easy to resolve? In this situation there is a total lack of control, while the "principle of pleasure" prevails.

Chapter 2

Who are the two protagonists of the dance of addiction?

The "Victim"

Let's start by saying that generally affective dependence is a phenomenon that in 99% of cases sees the woman as the protagonist of this problem. The literature shows that the age of the women involved is extremely variable, extending from the period of early adulthood (20-26 years) until reaching full adulthood (thus including women over 50 years with children even older). It is easy to think that socio-cultural elements (role of women in the male-centric society, prevalence of aggressive attitudes in the male figure ...) may have significantly affected the development and increase of affective relationships of dependence. However, avoiding coarse generalizations and entering the depths of the psychological aspects of women who suffer from this relational condition, we see that almost all of them have traits in common that help us better understand why they fall victim to this tormented "love": these are primarily women who manifest extreme emotional fragility and who very often spasmodically seek confirmation from their partner to be people of value and worthy of being loved. The image they have of themselves is therefore not particularly positive, on the contrary, they tend to have a low self-esteem and see their defects before their merits, often subjecting themselves to a very severe self-criticism.

Another characteristic that invasively permeates the lives of these women is the fear of abandonment: the fear of being abandoned by the partner becomes unsustainable and if such a situation were to occur, it could further reinforce the idea of not being worthy of the love of the other ("if he left me it is because I have something wrong", "he abandoned me as everyone in my life because I am worth nothing"). The tendency is therefore to attribute to themselves the responsibility for the good functioning of the couple. If the gears of the relational machine squeak, it means (in these women's minds) that they have not worked hard enough to make the relationship work optimally. Those who suffer from emotional dependence are unable or struggling to see the responsibilities of others for the proper functioning of the couple.

From the numerous studies that we find in the literature we can then discover that in many cases the emotional dependent comes from problematic families. Not infrequently In fact, in the past of these women there are situations of intra-family abuse, whether sexual, physical, or psychological. We discover that many of them had fathers or mothers who suffered from alcoholism or had other serious forms of addiction that affected family relationships in an extremely negative way. Sometimes it is enough that the parents (the most important reference figures for a child) do not meet the main needs of a child (safety, gratification, care, play, emotional sharing) to create a sense of inadequacy and NOT value that drags on into adulthood and leads to the firm belief that one is not worthy of being loved by others.

We have therefore seen that most of the time the Victim has a dependent personality that leads her to see only in others the sources of support and affection, which they cannot do without. Over time these people manage to consolidate this "lifestyle" and become true experts in choosing partners who are incapable of giving love.

But who is the other protagonist of this dance of addiction?

The "Narcissist"

Let's start by saying that often the other "dancer" is a person with very evident narcissistic personality traits. Sometimes, however, it is possible that the other member of the couple is a weak person, submissive but like the Narcissist can implement many manipulative behaviors, using this alleged weakness to put the partner in check. But let's see in detail who is the Narcissist.

These people have a grandiose sense of importance, often expecting others to recognize them as "superior" because of their supposed achievements or because of a phantom talent they think they possess. They fantasize too much about their own success, their own power and charm, their own beauty; they believe they are special, unique, and therefore deserve to hang out with high-class people. They need constant admiration and believe that everything is due to them and that others must fully meet their expectations and needs. They exploit others for their own purposes; they suffer from envy, are often arrogant and conceited and can even become aggressive if something hinders their planning. They completely lack empathy and therefore do not have the ability to "put themselves in each other's shoes".

Initially, people of this type can really exert a certain charm on others. Over time, however, this veil of appearance falls away and there remain deleterious, rude behavior, which tend to debase the partner creating high conflict within the couple.

What has been said can make you imagine people almost unscrupulous, more inclined to hurt the other to create a benefit for themselves than willing to love their neighbor. In fact, it is so. However, we must always consider that people of this type have a background of childhood and educational experiences that are sometimes made of emotional deprivation and sometimes of excessive attention. Sometimes they have suffered bereavement or abandonment at an early age; in some cases, they simply do not receive the love that every child would want from parental figures. Obviously, they are not excusing for dysfunctional behavior, but we always keep in mind that often behind certain attitudes or lifestyles are hidden suffering and discomfort. The Narcissist does not open to the other, he does not want to question himself or his own behaviors. The risk of damaging the beautiful and fascinating image that he has of himself (in essence a giant with clay feet) cannot be run and for this reason prefers to close himself emotionally to the world rather than suffer for having become aware of his own failure.

Chapter 3

Which are the personalities most predisposed to become dominant and dominated?

Cesare Lombroso, whose real name was Marco Ezechia, is considered the father of criminology. His idea was that a man's nature was written on his face, that there were criminals by birth (theory of the born criminal) and that the propensity to violence could be seen in the shape of a skull, in the teeth, in physiological deviations.

Later, with the evolution of criminology, his theses appeared at least bizarre and racist, because they were proposed, as causes of violence, the family and social environment in which the individual was born and lived. Now the time has come to restore value, at least partially, to his theories, considering the studies made on the brain of violent personalities.

But the reference to Lombroso in his essay considers the conformation of the brain associated with antisocial behavior. Studies indicate an incomplete development of the prefrontal cortex, an abnormality in the posterior cingulate cortex, amygdala, and hippocampus dysfunctions, which, while not giving rise to psychic disorders, may make a subject more likely to commit crimes.

The author demonstrates this by operating tomographies on the brain of prisoners or neuroimaging functional to violent husbands.

These results integrate the solely social perspective of post-Lombrosian criminology, stating that environmental contingencies act and extrinsic the genetic components especially in the first years of life.

Now we try to provide scientific evidence to previous theories. In fact, Raine affirms that an absent family environment, of abandonment or characterized by malnutrition can determine the onset of one or more of the brain defects described above. The damage also spreads during the prenatal period if the mother smokes, drugs, or drinks alcohol in large quantities during pregnancy.

Modern neurocriminology will in the future be able to offer a criminological profile from the earliest days of a child's life, using genetic, biological, and environmental parameters.

However, ethical dilemmas arise, because beyond the genes there is free will, so these people should not be stigmatized. Otherwise, what would happen to the concept of responsibility?

Instead, prevention must be encouraged in families at risk. In fact, an English study has shown that by teaching emotional, emotional, and assertive communication to children at an early age from kindergarten, antisocial behavior in genetically predisposed personalities could be prevented.

In addition, a prevention campaign should be carried out on mothers by teaching them correct habits in pregnancy and appropriate educational styles in the care of children.

Obviously, what has been written so far affects the family dynamics of psychological and physical violence against the victim and children.

This is demonstrated by Raine's research that, in addition to prisoners, analyze their violent husbands and partners.

Violence witnessed by children can lead over time to behavior that is ascribed to violence perpetrated or suffered.

In fact, victims of family violence can choose violent partners because they feel "at home" and unconsciously retrace the evolutionary stages experienced in the family. This explains why victims tend to choose and stay with the perpetrators, not reporting the violence suffered to the authorities and forgiving the partner, after a momentary abandonment of the relationship.

In addition to this, the victim could be suffering from a real personality disorder, for example, the dependent personality disorder, which manifests itself with a series of specific criteria which, when present with high frequency, constancy, and severity, pervasively affect many aspects of the individual's life (working life, friendly and sentimental relationships, sociality). The person "feels" that he or she must maintain at all costs personal relationships that give him or her the idea of never feeling, not even for a single moment, alone. The basic idea of these people is not being able to live alone, in total autonomy, because they do not think they can cope with the events that life puts in front of them (especially the negative ones). They have strong feelings of bewilderment and sometimes experience existential emptiness, almost as if their presence and life were useless without someone beside them.

To avoid possible abandonment by the other, these people do everything to ensure the presence of their partner, they try in a thousand ways to become indispensable to the person next to them in such a way as to prevent them from thinking of abandoning them. We therefore understand that these efforts are aimed at consolidating as much as possible the dependence on the partner and vice versa, because unfortunately they perceive their value in a negative way, underestimating their abilities. The type of thinking that these people do strongly affects their mental state, so much to induce moments of deep sadness that sometimes lead to depressive disorders.

It should be specified that people who suffer from addictive personality disorder (mostly women) have their own desires and needs, but they do not satisfy them if they are not strongly supported by their reference figures (friends, colleagues, parents, siblings) and their approvals.

The need for continuous confirmation from others, the fear of being abandoned, the inability to express one's own point of view and the continuous self-devaluations consequently compromise the working environment, friendship, and social relationships. If the person is self-employed, it will obviously be extremely difficult to make autonomous decisions without the continuous support of someone. If the person depends on someone, they will clearly be inclined to support any decision of their bosses, however wrong it may be, in order not to collide with them, even if this means developing a deep sense of exploitation and injustice.

Emotional dysregulation (also typical of other personality disorders such as borderline personality disorder) explains in some situations how the ability to tolerate negative emotions and moods and the difficulty to "exploit" positive emotions to effectively counteract the former. Negative emotions sometimes give rise to acting out, i.e., dysfunctional "behavioral acts" (suicidal thoughts, self-harm, compulsive drug abuse ...).

Emotional dysregulation and dissociation resulting from past traumas can make one hypothesize a link with the emotional addiction developed later in adulthood. Support this hypothesis recent studies carried out by Teicher et al.: the results of this study highlight the brain alterations of specific areas responsible for the regulation of emotions and needs in people who have suffered significant past trauma, giving support (now) to the etiopathogenetic hypothesis of childhood trauma in the formation of these disorders and their correlation. with emotional dependence.

This disorder can affect both victims and perpetrators of the abuse because, once reached adulthood, females who are affected tend to remain victims of violence, while males tend to perpetrate it.

However, while arousing interest in the scientific community, the issue is very controversial and debated, lending itself - according to some - to simulations difficult to ascertain. Moreover, if the disorder is diagnosed, it would lead to accuse the patient's family members of sexual abuse of young children, ruining their lives with an accusation not supported by another source of subsistence (McHugh and Martin Orne). According to others, those who discredit the existence of multiple personality disorder do so to minimize the social extent of the phenomenon of violence against children and the damage it creates (Lowenstein).

As you can well understand, the diagnosis of multiple personality disorder is certainly not simple, but it must be considered the possibility that there are negative personalities lurking outside the reach of our consciousness, which can take over our control at any time, and that this represents a serious and real threat. It must also be said that the idea of Dr. Jekyll and Mr. Hyde, if on the one hand, evokes anxiety, on the other hand, has always shown a certain obscure fascination.

Unlike theories, the objectivity of the problem arises in its entirety if the multiple personality disorder is to be assessed in a courtroom, either by the victim or the perpetrator. To demonstrate that at the time of the facts to suffer or to perform the act was one of the alter ego and that perhaps at the time of the debate he is not present does not remain an easy thing to say or to do, as well as to be able to attribute the mental illness.

Chapter 4

Affective manipulation and psychological and physical violence as effects of emotional addiction

First, we give a definition of the concepts expressed in the title of the chapter, to make it easier to understand the relational dynamics that belong to the dysfunctional couple:

Affective manipulation

We specify that anyone (friend, colleague, boyfriend) can be an emotional manipulator. So, we are talking about a person who, when he or she enters a relationship with the other, does not hesitate to exploit the weaknesses of the "target" subject to satisfy his or her own requests and needs. Everything is done through different strategies, instilling feelings of guilt in the other, using lies, pretending to be a victim, making the other feel a wrong person, in essence making the victim of such behaviors feel compelled to "repair" an alleged damage, doing as the emotional manipulator wants.

Often many of us understand by the term violence the behavior that, physically, concretely, through aggressiveness, causes bodily injury to another person. There are other forms of violence that create consequences sometimes even worse than physical violence. We speak for example of economic violence (exploiting a condition of economic advantage to subjugate the victim), cultural violence (people who for their own purposes make the other feel inferior by using their greater cultural capacity to subjugate them) and psychological violence. The latter highlights a set of attitudes that aim to devalue as much as possible the other person and the latter's way of being. The main objective is therefore to subdue the person for the satisfaction of one's own needs, making full use of the insecurities and weaknesses of the victim, taking advantage of low self-esteem, putting in place behaviors not particularly striking but frequent and above all constant over time (from the Latin proverb "a drop digs the rock"!). The "psychological rapist" is an expert in the use of humiliation and debasement, even reaching attitudes of obvious contempt towards the victim. Destructive criticism (even sometimes of a sexual nature) is another favorite tool of this kind of people, who want to induce shame in the victim, who often fails to react to these situations. Let us also remember that these attitudes can reach their peak through threats, intimidation and in any case all those behaviors that induce a strong sense of unease (anxiety) in people who are victims (think of the typical example of the stalker who makes extensive and abundant use of these techniques to induce terror in the designated victim). The goal of psychological violence is to create a situation of maximum control over the victim, making them feel completely dependent on their partner.

Women who experience these situations may feel imprisoned, unable to escape their "persecutor". Not infrequently psychological violence can induce a depressive state in the victims (due to the continuation of the violence and the feeling of helplessness they provoke), sometimes so severe that they create suicidal thoughts (which sometimes result in suicidal behavior).

Physical violence

By this term we mean all those behaviors that are intended to cause physical pain in the victim and/or even injury and that at the same time induce a state of discomfort, anxiety, and fear in the victim. For example, we think of pinching, slapping, punching and/or kicking someone, torturing, sevicing, biting, pushing, pulling hair, pulling by the neck, preventing a person from eating, being held by force, being threatened with a weapon (stick, knife, gun...), mutilating female genitals, burning with fire or acid, killing. Obviously varies the extent of the injuries, which can be simple abrasions or mutilation, deep wounds, bone fractures. The one who implements physical violence in some way wants to imprint his mark of dominion on the body of the other, wants to inspire fear to exercise control over the victim in an aggressive way (and we repeat that in most cases the victims are women).

These three seemingly different situations are well united by the purpose of subjugating the other, basing the report on the "power of control". Sometimes one wonders why the woman victim of manipulation and/or violence does not react. It is difficult to give a clear and unambiguous answer because considerations must be made on different levels. First, it is necessary to take into consideration the history of women (as we said in the initial chapter) and their evolution in relation to the tendency of the male gender to subject them to predetermined roles: today we can well see that, despite the progress made, there is always and, in any case, a basic tendency to consider women's abilities lower than those of men. Let's think for example in Parliament, where only in the last few decades pink quotas have increased (the number of female representatives in the

Chamber of Deputies and Senate), but there is still no fairness and balance (the number of representatives in Parliament is still for the vast majority of men). Let's think about the power (managerial) roles in large state and private companies, which for the most part is covered by male figures. In short, to "emerge" compared to men, women must work ten times as hard, on the one hand to demonstrate their skills and on the other to fight prejudices and stereotypes that concern them (and the result is not obvious).

Secondly, it is necessary to evaluate in which socio-cultural context the woman lives (this is correlated to what has been written above): there are, for example, countries (China) where the role of women, especially in rural environments and where the cultural level is poorly developed, is subjugated regardless of the couple relationship. In many contexts of Indian society there is a division by castes and within castes the role of women is sometimes submissive. In Iran, Iraq, and many other Middle Eastern countries is the religion that somehow regulates (sometimes in a fundamentalist way) the male and female roles. It is therefore essential to consider these factors when dealing with the issue of violence against women.

Third, it is necessary to enter the relational dynamics of the couple, to understand what the inhibitory brakes are, what are those situations that "brake" eventual reactions of the victim. For example, it is important to know that, even where there is the desire to "escape" from a difficult situation, often the disadvantaged economic conditions of the woman do not allow her alternatives and constrain her, not allowing her to immediately implement such a decision. When there are children, it becomes even more difficult to choose, because you are held back by the fear of repercussions on them, by the fear of losing them. The lower ability to react also depends on the physical capabilities of the woman, which are by nature different and different is the level of aggressiveness (which in men for historical-genetic factors is certainly higher). The condition of social isolation that is established over time in a sneaky and progressive way "takes away" social support to the victim, induces a state of loneliness and clouding the possible strategies and solutions to get out of the problem. When in the background there are feelings of affection towards the partner, there is always the hope that something can change, so you put yourself in a position of perpetual waiting, forgetting that a situation changes more quickly the more decisively we first implement a change in our behavior.

Clinical Cases

The case of Francesca

Francesca (fancy name) was 30 years old in 2015. Ten years earlier she had met Michele with whom, after four years of cohabitation, she got married, going to live in a rented house on the outskirts of Vicenza. Already a month after the wedding an unfortunate episode occurs when, at the wedding of a friend of theirs, during the banquet held at a Palladian villa, for a jokingly winking and certainly not vulgar photo that she had taken in public with another guest, after the party and just alone in the car on the way home, he says to her verbatim: "You're a slut, you suck and I want to separate", all seasoned with insults of various kinds. Once home, the man takes possession of their savings book, co-owned, thus preventing Francesca from accessing the contents and for a month they lead a life as "separated at home". This, considering that they were at the beginning of their marriage, causes her a strong state of frustration, so much so that she must leave the conjugal roof and return to her parents' house for a week.

However, to try to save the marriage, considering that she was in love, Francesca does everything to reconcile, until they return to live together. With all of this, the man, every day, has something to say about everything Francesca does, starting from shopping, how she tidies up the house, how she dresses, how she cooks: everything is wrong, and she is a "good-for-nothing, moron, idiot" and others of the same type.

This leads her to shut herself in herself, to cry in secret so as not to be mocked. Another habit of his is to check her cell phone, against her will, to find traces of men she was not aware of. A little at a time his propensity to humiliate her, from the private sector he begins to exercise it in public, so that often, in convivial occasions, in the presence of common friends or parents, he offers the same phrases and assumes the same vexatious attitudes. Begging or crying and requests to be less offensive and violent never do any good.

Even though, as said, the insults are now daily, trusting that with time his attitude is silent, Francesca still decides to stay with him, so much so that, after a year and a half, they buy together a house where they move. The move into the new home, however, does not change the situation and she, daily, continues to suffer his excesses, in private and in public, and crying in secret looking for a solution that, now in a state of serious psychological prostration, cannot find.

Direct witnesses of her state are above all her parents, who often witness the frequent episodes in which he offends her saying "Bitch, dickhead, slut, handicapped, you have to die", without justification. Never in all this time, perhaps held back by the guilt generated by the man, Francesca thinks of turning to the authorities to file a complaint for what she has suffered.

Almost two years pass when, by now at the end of her life, after a whole month of living together in which Michele never speaks to her, Francesca finds the courage to ask the man if he agreed to separate. He answers that he is thinking about it too, as she had never been a real wife as far as he was concerned, having made him miss everything even as a woman. After hearing a lawyer and deciding to proceed with a consensual separation, a couple of months later they arrive together in a hearing for their counterpart. They establish in the context that the house, with the furniture, is sold and, after paying the mortgage, the remainder divided in half. Nothing was decided about who and when to vacate the house. They continue to live together, except for a few weekends and a few other days when she stays at her parents' house, where she also stays overnight.

On these occasions Michele, whose behavior was now aimed at ignoring her or some impromptu insult, begins to call her dozens of times on her cell phone; in some days he arrives to do so more than forty times in twenty-four hours and to send her more than twenty sms daily. His requests to stop are worthless.

Starting from this period, Michele's aggressiveness, and his forms of control over Francesca increase significantly, culminating in serious episodes of physical violence. To better understand his forms of control, significant is what happened in the following month, when Francesca receives a contact on her Facebook page from a self-styled "Andrea" (surname omitted), already known among her social network friends, with whom she had correspondence. Only after a week Francesca learns that that name hides Michele who, as it turns out, calls her a "slut" and more, for chatting with a stranger.

The day after this episode, while Francesca is at the commune's house, checking against her will - as she often did - her cell phone, Michele finds the number of a man she doesn't know and insists to know who he is. To Francesca's answer that he is a common acquaintance, Michele insults her by calling her a "slut" and slaps her in the face, so much so that he forces her to go to the hospital emergency room, since this episode exacerbates the symptoms of a heart disease that the woman suffers from and of which the persecutor is perfectly aware. Michele, reached her while she was still at the hospital, approached her and said: "You are not so bad ... you can sign to go home", which the girl, completely succubus, does, having no other place to go and not wanting to give the late hour wake up her parents, giving them further cause for concern.

Arrived at home he reiterates, as he always did, that his reaction was also this time due to a fault of her, as she had allowed herself to make the acquaintance of other people without informing him. Finally, however, Francesca matures the idea of abandoning the marital roof, a project that she wants to realize trying not to oppose too much Michele, fearing to suffer, in addition to the psychological violence to which she was accustomed, even physical violence, which would have aggravated her state.

So, she began to gradually transfer her personal belongings to her parents' house, trying to ignore the usual insults of the man. In the time that follows, whenever she leaves the house or stays with relatives, Michele the storm of dozens and dozens of calls and as many text messages with which he continues to blame her for all matters even not related to their relationship. This causes her a serious state of anxiety and stress that affects her life, upsetting her sleep/wake rhythm, her relationships with others and deconcentrating her workplace as an employee.

In this transitional period, before the final transfer to her parents (another two months had passed by then), when Michele received a message on her cell phone, after having insulted her with the usual insulting epithets and said that she should not exchange sms with her friends, he hit her violently in the face with slaps. Painful, escaping her violence, Francesca still goes to the emergency room, where she is medicated. This fact, however, finally determines her definitive estrangement from the marital home to go and live with her parents.

Thus, begins a period in which Michele floods her with dozens and dozens of phone calls and as many text messages. So, spend another two months in which the two do not meet, until she goes to the former marital home to deliver to Michele half of the amount to pay a bill. Since Michele is still missing 15 euros to pay the full amount due, he, after starting to film her with his cell phone, very aggressively screams - lying - that she had not given him any amount of money and that she had to sign a declaration in which she admitted that she wanted to leave the marital roof spontaneously.

Frightened and mindful of the physical violence already suffered, Francesca asked for the intervention of the Carabinieri, who arrived on the scene with a patrol. In the presence of the military Michele denies that the girl ever delivered the money she owed him and states that he would have denounced her, as he falsely accused him of having beaten her in the previous days.

She manages to get away thanks to the intervention of the military, for a period Francesca avoids Michele, who however continues to harass her with calls and sms. After another ten days, the surprise is shocking when one evening she finds him waiting for her outside the company where she works. The man has arrived with his car and is waiting for her standing outside the car. Francesca, as soon as she sees him, rushes to his car parked not far away and closes the car inside, forgetting to open a small window. He creeps into the crevice with one arm and, apparently calm, tells her about the episode in which the Carabinieri had intervened, asking her if we could remain friends and telling her she could keep their house for six months of the year. In doing so, however, he prevents her from making any manoeuvre to move away, since the car was parked among others and, if it had moved, given its position it would have caused him serious injuries, since he did not want to remove the arm from where he had placed it. So, he forces her to listen to his chatter for an hour, until finally he leaves.

In the following days Michele continues to harass her with phone calls and messages to which, as for the previous ones, Francesca answers very few and only when they concern concrete matters related to their home and related matters.

Another ten days have passed since the last meeting, after having harassed her with sms and phone calls to which

She doesn't answer, around one o'clock in the morning Michele arrives at the house of Francesca's parents, where she lives and at the moment absent. She sticks to the bell ringing several times, and then leaves after about half an hour, getting no answer. This fact, combined with the absence of her parents, terrifies her, so much so that she locks herself in the house, barring doors and windows, but unable to sleep all night, considering that place is no longer safe for her safety. This, in the following days, was followed by hundreds of phone calls and text messages to which Francesca did not answer, except for a phone call in which Michele - as announced by a message sent to Francesca's father - reported that he needed a certificate necessary to proceed with the sale of the common house. As soon as he heard the voice of her, the man, completely neglecting the supposed reason for the conversation, shouted out to her: "It's time to stop, you slut!!!". She hangs up.

Another subsequent episode concerns a series of messages received, in which Michele says that, by mistake, with the car he had broken a painting from a series of three paintings given to them by her father and that they were still at what had been the old marital home. Sorrowful for what happened, at her suggestion, Francesca proposes to give him the author's number, to have it reproduced. To this Michele replies that it was a joke and that she should have known, since the paintings "...she had already taken them..." and therefore she could not falsely accuse him of having done something wrong with those paintings. Of course, that was not true since those canvases were still with him.

After another month, finally Francesca, together with her father and a cousin, went to the former residence to collect her personal belongings. Preventively she warned Michele that she would come by, to avoid that he could have to complain or complain about the lack of objects of his property. There arrived, while Francesca takes care of taking what he owns, Michele follows her step by step throughout the house, insulting her: "Slut, whore you and your mother, slut, gypsy, beggar, you are an abortion of a woman unable to give me a child, who knows if a tumor will come to you and your father" and other of the same tenor.

At a certain point the man, after having violently closed the entrance door of the apartment with the excuse of preventing the cat from getting out and leaving her companions outside, while they are alone inside a room, tears from her hands a box emptying its contents on the floor and hit her repeatedly with it. Francesca starts screaming "help", while he approaches a window with his hands up, saying out loud that he was "not doing anything" to her. The girl takes advantage of this moment of distraction to run out of the house, while her father asks the Carabinieri to intervene. Michele told the soldiers who had arrived that he had done nothing and that inexplicably she had slammed the front door of the apartment several times and dropped a box. Moreover, always for no reason, she had started to shout for help. However, the police remain until the completion of the moving operations.

In the following days, the telephone persecution continues by Michele, who repeatedly appears, even in the middle of the night, at her parents' house, shouting from the street and repeatedly ringing the bell. On these occasions the police are alerted, and Michele manages to escape from them by leaving before his arrival.

Having reached the end of her life, Francesca finally relies on a psychotherapist and presses charges.

Comments

From this reading, which induces a state of anxiety in the reader, it can be seen how the dominant person acts on the victim and what the victim suffers from through manipulations that will be described in more detail.

amply in the second part of the book and how, once the latter decides to close the relationship, the manipulative aspect does not end, but rather leads to physical violence and persecutory behavior.

It must be considered, as already reported in many parts of the book, that the aspects within which these situations mature are already pre-existing. In Francesca's case, a dependent personality certainly facilitated the meeting with Michele and the decision to go and live with him, even though during the engagement period it became clear that there was certainly no "healthy love" at the basis of their relationship. In fact, the intolerance for an unsatisfactory life lived in the family of origin and the desire to leave favoured in her the choice to marry Michele despite everything. The manipulation of him was interpreted by the victim as interest and love for her, thus reinforcing the behavior of the executioner who, in this case, became a surrogate for his father.

In the second part of the text will be given some advice on how to act more effectively in case of separation.

The case of Giorgio

To make, as far as possible, the tension produced on the victim by a manipulative and persecutory attitude more perceptible to the reader and, at the same time, to try to identify and understand the "dark" forces that motivate the author, we report an episode in which the protagonists, for once with roles reversed from those commonly known, are a man and a woman: Giorgio and Cristina.

About a year ago, Giorgio was hired with a twelve-month project contract at a public office. Here he met Cristina, an employee at that office, where he worked with a colleague of his. Sometime later, after entering formal confidence, Cristina approaches him saying that she is a "medium" and that she can act as an intermediary with his father, who had died a few years before. To make herself credible, given Giorgio's ill-concealed perplexity with her statement, she claims to have been contacted some time before by the Carabinieri of a Lombard province to help them track down a missing woman. On that occasion she had reported to the military that she was dead, which then turned out to be true.

During the interview he had on that occasion, inside the office where they work, she told him that if he wanted her help to communicate with his father, it was enough for him to bring her a photo and they would get in touch with him. Of course, while thanking her for her concern, Giorgio did not accept. This episode does not change their normal professional cohabitation, even if sometimes Giorgio notices that she was excessively kind and caring.

About six months later, on Easter, Cristina gives him an envelope with inside a sheet of paper with the sentence "Happy Easter - I love you - greetings to your mother. Daddy". Although perplexed, in order not to displease the woman given the shared working relationship, Giorgio accepts the envelope and its contents, putting them away without thinking about it further.

After about a month, one Saturday afternoon Cristina calls him on his cell phone asking him if he could help her, because she was stuck in the city center because she couldn't start her bike anymore. Out of courtesy duty, Giorgio reaches her solving the problem.

In the following days, saying that the bike was no longer suitable for her, she stubbornly wanted to sell it to Giorgio. After a short period of time, the man agrees to go out one evening to go to a ballroom, which ends with a one-hour chat outside the club, at the presence of friends.

In the following days, Cristina tries to involve him in the purchase of a new motorcycle and Giorgio, to stop his insistence, advises her on which model to buy, finally accompanying her to the dealer to pick it up. Until this moment the relationships are maintained in the context of "favors between colleagues". However, Giorgio notes that, more and more often, she speaks out loud about her personal matters with her other colleague.

In particular, she often says that "she was tired of her husband and hoped that he would leave home so that she could finally find a younger man". If on the one hand it seems improbable to him, on the other hand he perceives that such phrases could in fact be pronounced for "her benefit" because, at the same time, the woman is particularly full of attention to him: among other things, she often bakes cakes at home that she brings to the office and gives him or leaves him chocolates and cards with "kisses" written in the desk drawer.

Their relationship, however, maintains a rather formal line until, around the middle of the same month, out of the blue, Cristina comes out with this invitation: "Why don't you and I start dating for a while?". Giorgio replies that he doesn't feel like it, coming from a relationship that has just ended. However, she insists that "If it doesn't work, there would be no problem".

Given his obstinacy, to the new insistence of the woman who continues to demand another date together, Giorgio accepts another appointment. This is repeated for another five/six times, with an interval of about a week from each other. On these occasions they meet in outdoor places, such as squares, or at freeway toll booths parking lots. Here they limit themselves to chatting about the more and the less remaining in the car. Each of the meetings does not last more than two hours and only in one of these they exchange caresses in intimacy, without however reaching a complete sexual intercourse.

However, this attendance, forcibly accepted by Giorgio, does not gratify him, so after another month begins to systematically decline the invitations to go out together that continue to arrive from Cristina.

In the meantime, the "forced" relationship reduces Giorgio's productivity in the working environment, so much so that he is moved from the office he shares with the woman to an adjacent one, where another employee works. This change in logistics rarefies the occasions of meeting with Cristina, whose contacts in the professional field are now limited to greetings while, as far as personal relationships are concerned, after another couple of outings they stop meeting. It is then that she sends him a text message saying that "...her husband had left home, leaving her everything, that now he no longer had to hide and that he too would stop being a stopgap, becoming a future love...". Giorgio does not answer but notes the strange "coincidences" with which the woman tries to have "close contacts": she often walks down the corridor passing in front of the office where he is, waits for him at the coffee vending machines, leaves work earlier than the end of her shift, but at the same time as the end of Giorgio's shift and more.

In August he leaves for vacation, living this moment as a liberation; he receives only one text message from Cristina, with which she asks him when he would return to work. At his return to the office, after three weeks, he finds Cristina waiting for him at the entrance; after a couple of days, she calls him to ask him to go away for two days with his camper and he answers with a definite "no".

At the end of the month, in the early afternoon, Cristina shows up at Giorgio's house on a vintage moped. When the doorbell rang, Giorgio's mother - 72 years old - answers the intercom, who, at the suggestion of her son, present in the house, asked her the following question replies that the man was in bed resting. Cristina replies that it doesn't matter and that she would have waited for him out there. After about fifteen minutes, since the dog, aware of Cristina's presence in front of the gate had started barking and harassing the whole neighborhood, Giorgio went down to the street. As soon as she saw him, Cristina said to him: "I brought you this..." and handed him the keys to the scooter, which he knew he liked very much. He refuses them decisively and invites her to leave, hinting at going back into the house. Surprising him with her dexterity, the woman grabs his hand and kisses her. He withdraws and leaves. As soon as he comes back, she insists on the intercom bell, forcing him to go out again. As soon as he sees her again, she says to him: "Forgive me". Giorgio replies that he forgives her, but that now he must leave and never return. At this point, after having lingered a little longer, Cristina goes away. The next day, in the office, Giorgio confronts her, telling her not to behave like that anymore; she doesn't answer.

After a few days and having arrived to the penultimate one of work (as said, Giorgio's was a project contract), while he is at the desk intent on doing, Cristina enters the room and grabs him violently by the head and the neck trying to kiss him. Not being able to free himself from the grip and to avoid creating embarrassment to the other two colleagues present, to mask the situation by softening the tones, the man gives a kiss on the woman's cheek, saying: "Cristina, see that we have time to say goodbye tomorrow too". This induces Cristina to let go of her grip whispering: "I did it out of love" and to return to her office. The tension, however, is palpable, but everyone pretends nothing. At this point, however, Giorgio goes to her office, who is alone and calmly begs her not to do it again.

Back to his station, after a couple of minutes he is reached again by the woman, who behaves in the same way. This time, he rejects her decisively, asking for help from the other two colleagues as well, help that is not necessary anyway, managing to free himself. Cristina, after this further attempt to kiss him, saying incomprehensible words to him, moves away, and then comes back after three more minutes and again in the same attitude. Screaming for help, Giorgio manages this time to break away and escape down the stairs, chased by her. Other employees, attracted by the hustle and bustle and the screams, witness the fact. He hides behind a telephone booth, thus managing to watch her chasing him. As soon as Cristina goes out to look for him in the parking lot, he goes up the stairs, locking himself in an office at his spare time, where he tries, though understandably shaken, to resume work. However, the computer installed in this room doesn't work, so he goes back to the original workstation closing, with the complicity of the colleagues, the door with key to avoid the repetition of the unpleasant episodes just described. In the meantime, Cristina came back and sat in front of the closed door, trying, from time to time, to open it. After about an hour that they were locked inside, the section manager and one of her collaborators arrived, in the meantime called. Let them in, they are immediately pressed by Cristina, who, with difficulty, continues to insistently repeat: "I only did it out of love...".

Since then, Giorgio no longer meets his harasser at work, but she does not give up in her persecutory actions. Two days after the facts just told, an average of 6/7 sms per day begins to arrive on his cell phone, to which he does not answer. These messages contained love phrases, combined with incomprehensible mystical references.

After four more days, Cristina and her son Alex return to Giorgio's home. He hides in the garden, while she talks to her mother saying: "I am a medium" (sentence confirmed by her son), "her son is about to die; I came to take him to the hospital immediately". In that context, she also shows a letter, which says that she wants to deliver personally to Giorgio. The mother, a widow, bleaches in prey to a negative emotion too strong while Cristina, imperturbable, asks her to call her son, who does not answer the phone. The old woman, having gained courage, answers that Giorgio doesn't show up with her anymore either, at which point the two leave. The next day Giorgio goes to the police station to ask how to behave and receives some advice.

After two days, at about 8.00 p.m., her son returns to Giorgio's house, rings and, at the invitation to leave, leaves in the mailbox a letter written by Cristina "under the guidance of her deceased father", who would have said that Giorgio had to trust her and love her.

After two more days, without any message to accompany him, the molested man finds in the mailbox of the house a large "hunting" knife that, in that moment, he remembers to have already seen in Cristina's possession in the period in which they worked together, of which he knows that the woman is used to carry it in her bag for "self-defense". She had in fact noticed it also on their first outing, whose details have already been reported. At that time, he had invited her to leave it at home, since the carrying of weapons is against the law. He took the knife, carefully grabbing it and put it in a nylon bag and kept it in the house. The day after the discovery, among others, he receives a text message from Cristina in which she asks him if he liked it.

Subsequently, on average every other day, Giorgio finds in the mailbox of the house letters without postage and address. In the contents, all similar, some of them reported love and pseudomistic sentences, in which Cristina refers to the feeling she felt for him and the desire to be together, all interspersed with religious/Christian quotations, while others were the result of the "medium" function exercised by the woman and the words reported those "suggested" by Giorgio's deceased father, who urged him to listen to Cristina and to love her.

After two days the man finds in the mailbox a similar package to the previous ones, with inside, besides the writing, also a crucifix. Another day the letter also contains a multi-purpose knife.

After another three days, in a further envelope/letter found, he notices inside an object that he cannot identify. He then calls 113, who sends a steering wheel whose operators retrieve the envelope and check its contents: in addition to the usual writing, there was a corkscrew! The reasons for the presence of this object were not explained. On the same day, shortly before the discovery of this envelope, Giorgio had called Cristina to admonish her to stop her seriously harassing behavior. The answer of this last one had been a resounding laughter, followed by a sms with written "be on your guard". The next day Giorgio changed the number of his cell phone.

If she no longer receives messages, however, the letters continue to arrive. In one with the writing, he received a bunch of keys that Cristina says are those of her scooter and her house. In the message she claims that the next day, at 5 p.m., Giorgio shows up at her house; obviously, the man does not comply.

The next day, Cristina searches for him several times on his fixed users, managing to talk to his mother who, when asked where he was, answers that he does not live in that house anymore and that she does not have to look for him at that address anymore.

Useless effort, as Cristina ignores the invitation following to call him even at night.

It is here that a new fact happens Giorgio is contacted by the manager of the public office where he had worked, who invites him to call a psychiatrist of the local ASL because

The latter wanted to be informed about the events that happened between him and Cristina when he was still employed. Called and informed, the doctor says that he would have proceeded in relation to the request of the employer but limited to the importance of the woman's ability to perform her job, without entering the merits of any psychological suffering of which she could be affected.

After a couple of days to Giorgio, in the usual mailbox, comes another envelope with inside, besides the usual love/medianic and mystic-religious letters, the keys of Cristina's house and the invitation to go to her the next day.

At this point, supported also by the service offered by the association "Volere è Potere", Giorgio presents a complaint. The woman in first instance has been convicted for persecutory behavior and awaits the outcome of the appeal.

Comments

The narrated episode highlights the multiplicity of manipulative systems that can be used on the victim by leveraging his weaknesses and difficulties. Giorgio, in fact, suffered the loss of his father, to whom he was overly attached, and the loneliness of his mother. Cristina, having understood this, acted by manipulating him and passing herself off as a "medium".

It must be considered the involvement in the situation of third people, his elderly mother, and her children and the condescension of the latter towards their mother's manipulative behavior, of which they were also unwittingly victims. Which adults will they be?

The systems to manipulate may be the most disparate and imaginative, but the result is the same: to keep the victim hooked and produce suffering, as the story of the case wanted to evoke.

It is not only men, therefore, who dominate, but also women, with more subtle but no fewer devastating methods. Giorgio had lost ten kilos and suffered from anxiety and panic.

The case of the victim-defendant

From a superficial evaluation the victim-defendant oxymoron, as two aspects of the same subjectivity, could appear out of context to validate or not the presence of a manipulation hypothesis. Moreover, it could appear even more original if it concerns the exploitation of the affection nurtured by parents towards a daughter. However, the case reported below confirms what has been stated, a hypothesis that is not considered relegated only to sporadic events.

As we will see, the one that from a first analysis could pass as the victim, is the author of a plan, elaborate, aimed at involving, despite himself and in a negative sense, the one who does not meet his expectations, trying to gain a "secondary advantage".

At the basis of this behavior, of course, there is a deep psychic suffering, but sometimes it is so well hidden that even the shrewdest can be deceived.

Clara and Matt, after a brief love affair, separated on the latter's decision. If at first, she willingly accepts the solution of the relationship, after a few months she begins to storm the young man with messages and phone calls to convince him to get back together. Matt, categorically declined the invitation and tired of being

harassed, change phone users. After a few weeks, getting no more answer, Clara shows up at the boy's house together with his mother who, having found his parents, starts to insult them by telling them that they had not raised their children well, Matt and Lorence, because the first one molested his daughter by sending dozens of daily text messages and the second one had first had the girl give him a gold necklace of great value and then he had made himself unavailable to avoid returning it. The woman claims to have noticed the numerous messages received on her daughter's cell phone and the disappearance of the necklace.

The parents of the boys, stunned, deny any accusation, and reserve the right to inquire. From that day on, Clara's father began to call Matt's house repeatedly, repeating to him and his parents what his wife had already told him; the defenses of Matt's father and mother, who, convinced by their children's justifications, deny the disputed facts, are useless.

The situation drags on for a few days, after which Clara's parents and Matt's parents decide for a clarifying meeting to be held "de visu" in a neutral place, the "Youth House" of the country. During the meeting, Clara's parents confirm their accusations and show the girl's cell phone, where hundreds of text messages "signed" with Matt's name were present. To the decisive denial of the father and the mother of the latter, who assure that the telephone numbers from which the messages were received had never been available to the family (version then verified as reliable), Clara's parents leave furiously, claiming to believe their daughter and the evidence exhibited by her, and warning that they would immediately go to the Carabinieri to denounce the "theft" of the necklace operated by Lorenzo and the stalking practiced by Matt.

The judicial action reveals, among the elements of evidence, that the telephone cards from which the harassing messages to Clara had started were in her name and that the necklace of which they had lost track was from the girl sold in a shop not far from the town of residence.

What is surprising, however, is that despite the evidence, the girl has always continued to deny her direct involvement in the family as an author and that the parents, even during the trial that followed, have supported the innocence of their daughter, justifying the events as a hoax.

But this is not so much the real problem, as the inability of those two parents, despite themselves, to realize the discomfort of the daughter they love, but do not know.

The case of Margherita

The following story wants to represent, if still necessary, how there are no limits to the epilogue that can have a story to which an unbalanced and "sick" emotional relationship can lead. If the protagonists belong to a "world" that lives a bit on the margins of the so-called "normal" society, it is also true that the story comes at a time when the age of the actors had already reached an advanced maturity, just as everything comes after a period of cohabitation in which the couple had long been married and had two grown-up children.

It is possible that the psychological substratum of both spouses had always deteriorated, with unresolved dysfunctions because never analyzed, but the manifestation of the phenomena began when both were more than forty-five years old.

Ivano and Margherita were married in their early twenties. Average license he, who with his brother has a small goldsmith's workshop, while she is a housewife and, in addition to raising the children, helps him in the activity

craftswoman. Ivano is not particularly good at dealing with customers, so it is Margherita, more pragmatic, to manage the commercial part. Things go well until a period of crisis arrives. The economic difficulties that follow lead to the dissolution of the company with his brother and Ivano starts to work as a goldsmith's broker, using from time to time the workshop for small jobs.

However, the economic situation is further compromised: the work is little, and the debtors are late in paying. So Ivano begins to make small scams that lead him to be invicted to the goldsmith world, so much so that the usual suppliers stop entrusting him with tasks. The underground world remains, which in the sector is substantial but, as we know, just as risky. He receives and works with precious metals of dubious origin, but above all he begins to consume cocaine. Margherita tries to dissuade him from doing so, but it is he who drags her down the slope he has taken she too becomes a cocaine addict and helps him sell the substance, an activity he has in the meantime undertaken to deal with creditors and satisfy their dependence.

The moment arrives when Ivano is arrested for drug dealing and is investigated for a series of swindles used against goldsmith entrepreneurs. She is also investigated but does not go to jail. When he is released from prison, he engages in several illegal activities, but mainly drug dealing. What is more important, however, is that he is fierce against her: insults and physical and psychological violence. In particular, he develops a series of paraphilias that he imposes on his partner, forcing her to engage in sexual intercourse at the limit of the severity, even with the use of "tools" of all kinds. This is associated with the increase for both in the intake of cocaine and the increasingly devastating economic conditions in which the whole family finds itself.

From all this Margherita is strongly prostrated, but she is unable to leave the man; what she does, however, is to send her two children to live with their grandparents to preserve them, as far as possible, from the context.

Ivano is now exclusively engaged in dealing and is arrested again, but he perseveres. Margherita, who remains close to him in any case, is subjected against her will to any sexual desire on the part of the man, who forces her to have sexual relations with strangers she meets at toll booths, in highway parking lots or in places frequented by swingers.

Addicted to drugs and humiliated physically, exhausted the strength to oppose, Margherita will take her own life.

The one told, including the epilogue, is part of a story lived on the margins, but how many other "margins" exist and are not visible?

Other cases

Below you will read true stories that the protagonists, safeguarding privacy, wanted to share with you readers.

The story of Cristina

When we met, he made me believe that he had so much knowledge about diseases, because he said he had studied four and a half years of medicine (which is not true). I was about to go into treatment for anorexia and he said he understood me because he suffered from anxiety and depression. He listened to me and showed empathy towards me.

When our son Franco was little, he often took him to his parents saying that I needed to rest. When he could attend the nursery, he did not want to because he said that his parents would suffer not to keep him with them. Ditto for the nursery school, because it had to be a school close to his parents, even though we did not live nearby. Surely there were other good nursery schools, but Marco told me that his parents would have little way to go. Moreover, according to my in-laws, Franco had to stay with them until Marco finished working in the office to take him home.

Of course, when Franco started first grade, he only had lunch in the canteen a few times, because he had to go to his grandparents' house during his lunch break. Their choice was justified by saying that the child did not like what they served in the canteen at lunchtime. And so, Marco and his parents could pick him up and take him home, as the school was close to their home. After all, my partner had already had lunch with his parents for many years.

Franco always stayed with his grandparents after school and, when I wanted to pick him up, my in-laws said that Marco would pick him up after work.

At my protests, my ex (because he has become such) always told me that if I left him, I could never have the baby and that he would change the locks of the house. This happened.

He necessarily wanted to buy a house, but our economic conditions were difficult, so I had to work. On the one hand he seemed to love my parents, but on the other hand he always said to me: "You in Sweden do this and that... but here in Italy it's not good". The difference in culture was never accepted. His parents always told me that it did not make sense to speak Swedish to my son and to Franco his paternal grandmother used to say: "But what does the mother say that I don't understand that language!".

Thinking back today to Marco's behavior, it seems to me that he did everything just to keep me close to him, because I think he deeply knew that our story could not work. He never accepted me and always said that I was not a nice person. When I left him, he turned me against my son, who refused to see me for a long time. In conclusion, the psychological violence spread to extremes.

Reflection: the psychological violence directed at the former partner ends, unfortunately, to affect the innocent children.

The story of Valeria

My name is Valeria, I am 29 years old and about five years ago I met a boy, Alberto, of the same age as me. I, a quiet, sunny, touchy, thoughtful person, from a simple family, had decided to take a completely different career path from what my family had done. He was exuberant, self-confident, instinctive, of a well-to-do peasant family. At the time I was in the process of obtaining a freelance professional qualification, he was a farmer.

There was a feeling from the beginning... I noticed that I had to keep an eye on him, because of the girls around him, because he was a bit too extrovert if they gave him attention... But it was an aspect I could tame.

After three months, physical problems took over for me, which led me to a hospitalization of almost a month and his presence had become fundamental, even for the subsequent recovery, in which I was very encouraged. And the fact that he was close to me after such a short time that we were

We knew each other, I was awfully close to him.

After another three months a serious health problem happened to my mom. Here too his presence proved to be fundamental to deal with the situation, but I was beginning to see his intolerance to my pain for something/somebody who was not him.

He was not affectionate (he said he never received a hug from his parents, who rewarded him for his abilities with material goods), but he wanted affection and attention from me. As much as I could I tried to make him affectionate towards me, explaining to him what I liked too, but he did it for short periods, then everything went back to focusing on himself.

His affection showed it to me by buying me whatever I wanted, but it was not what I wanted!!!

The first year went well, I could not see or notice any flaws.

From the second year on, the problems began...and his true character emerged...a centralizer, an exhibitionist, and above all to my detriment. With the others he was extremely helpful. At times he was also extremely helpful with me, but probably they were moments of failure!!!!

I was suffering from his impatience and the jerks of nerves (never violent) agitated me, so I got nervous too.

I started, unfortunately, to look at his phone and with hindsight I can say that it was from there that the problems started: I could see that he said one thing to me and then he did another. I felt like I was being mocked.

After three years of history, I still wanted to give a shake to our relationship, also to evaluate if the story could continue and what it would have been like if we had lived together: both convinced, we went to live together, for rent, in an apartment in his country, because his work did not allow him (in his opinion) to move away. The first months were a disaster: different habits, quarrels about what are called "nonsense", but they are not, because it is from the small things that you can see how a relationship works.

His wanting to be the center of attention to my detriment made us quarrel with his childhood friends. I wanted him to face this problem, but it was not so, so I decided, after several attempts to overlook it, not to want to go out with them anymore, to avoid feeling "the laughingstock" of the group; I imposed this choice to him too, in his opinion correct.

The quarrels and my tears continued...because his attitude continued with other people, of course!!!! I avoided the problem, but not solved it.

He always told me to stay calm, because I was too nervous, and he could not bear to see me crying. He did not ask himself why I was crying!!!

He was more and more concentrated on his work, and I began to concentrate on my things...and that made him nervous. I begged him to help me at home (in my chores), to have more time for us, but nothing.

He would come home in the evening and, apart from cooking (making me weigh myself then that he did it, because he demanded that at eighteen o'clock I was at home, even though he knew very well what kind of work I was doing and even though he saw how much I was doing when I got home) and throwing out the garbage (often I had to remind him), then he would go to bed and watch TV and even this was cause for quarrel, because I wanted attention too.

The only time he was affectionate and sweet was in the morning when, before going to work, he would sit by our bed, hugging and kissing; it was our most beautiful moment.

His exhibitionism always prevailed more and more: never a stance in my favor... And sometimes I was ashamed of him, of what he said when we were in public. Megalomaniac. He knew everything, I observed that he wanted the looks of others only on him.

After a year of living together I left, but I came back to him after a month because he swore to me that he had understood the mistake and that it would never happen again. Once back, at first, he was all thoughtful and sorry, then he took the offended part because I had left.

After six months in my family there were health problems and again, I found myself in need of him, but even this time I often had to ask him to stay close to me, he supported me, verbally more than physically, but then he made me weigh it or at least he wanted to be reciprocated immediately.

I began to move away even physically, as I felt almost like an object. So, I thought about leaving him, but personal and family difficulties led me to want to have someone at my side to face the situation with more strength. In fact, at Easter of that year new health problems in my family took over and I had an immense need for affection and reassurance. But he was more and more impatient with this situation. Not feeling serene to be away from my father's home, I asked him to move us momentarily near my home country, so that the thought for my mother would be less pressing.

I always sought dialogue, I always explained to him my weaknesses and what was bothering me and making me suffer. I often told him to be honest with me, and that, in my opinion, he needed a woman like his mother, but he denied it undeterred and this made me believe in his possible change.

It was not a constructive coexistence and I believe more and more that he simply and slowly wanted to lead me to become like his mother.

There is no worse deaf than those who do not want to hear.

Hence the collapse and the closure of the relationship, for which I still wonder: "But who was really Alberto?".

Reflection: the manipulator unfortunately, has many faces and from this story we can see the strong disorientation of the victim, which is summarized in the final sentence of the story.

The story of Emily

"The best is yet to come," he would say whenever he gave me a lavish gift or planned a trip for two.

That was his classic answer. In the first six months.

In the remaining six (the relationship lasted a year and two weeks), I realized that the "best" was for him, not for me. Upon returning from a trip, I noticed how he criticized, in the form of "advice" (ergo, "lo-dico-per-te", n.d.a.), my work, how I spent my time and everything else. On Saturday afternoons, for example, he would ask me: "Come on, don't we always do what I like, what would you like to do? Then, on those rare occasions, with my dying desire to live, I would propose something. They didn't have time to spend two hours that already began the criticism about my choice of the "diversion" on Saturday afternoon. And every Saturday was the same story; in the end I stopped proposing the "diversions", so I didn't have to argue and then get upset.

I have always been a strong woman, who faced everything on her own and achieved her goals on her own. I am 32 years old, and I have achieved many goals. But that love that I had not received from my parents had led me to look for someone who loved me not for as I am, but for what I did, for my notoriety and for my appearance, because until today I have always thought that I, the love I had to deserve, like the degrees, the awards, the recognitions... In short, love was like anything else that in my existence and in my career required a certain amount of talent, self-denial, and perseverance. That's how I fell into its trap. I believed that, for the first time, someone loved me for who I was and not because I was the best, the most beautiful or the most loving. But unfortunately, it was not like that. For him I was a trophy to show off; I was revenge on love itself, since his first marriage had been a total failure. A stain on his beautiful narcissist resume. I was the "proof" that he had not made a mistake, because he had found something better.

That "something-better", that is me, one day was the object of heavy verbal attacks. I left, because I had never offended him, and I did not deserve those offenses.

On that occasion he used the strategy of silence. For a week he didn't make himself heard; then, suddenly, he called me. It was Christmas Eve, and I hadn't heard from him for seven days.

He showed up at my house, with the usual sumptuous gift. He never "officially" apologized to me. His apology was that object.

In the week he hadn't been in touch I thought it was over (I still didn't know the strategy of the "eternal return of the narcissist"), and I decided to get a dog. The dog of my dreams, to be exact. At first, he seemed not to blink when, at his "return", I explained to him that I would take the puppy anyway, even if he doesn't like dogs (he was afraid that they would ruin his furniture). But he wanted a child; evidently, he doesn't know what his children do to furniture.

... But the best was yet to come.

The two months between the first discussion (or rather, between his first episode of verbal violence) and the arrival of my puppy seemed to flow quietly. Certainly, with the ups and downs that a bipolar personality like hers contemplates.

Her desire to have a child had grown exponentially, almost as if to "compensate" for the arrival of my puppy. Of the series "I give you what you have chosen, but I want something else in return".

I would have liked to get married, before having a child. I have always been a very believing person and my dream has always been to get married in church (which I would have had to give up, if I had married him, since he was divorced). I would have made this (umpteenth) sacrifice for him. But having a child outside of marriage, at the age of 32, seemed excessive to me. I deserved more.

So, I pointed it out to him, and, at that point, a slow and exhausting defeat began, that is the "best, that was yet to come".

During the umpteenth discussion, at a time when I was very psychologically and emotionally rehearsed, he launched his final attack. He put his hands on me, left me unconscious, and fled like a thief.

Since that day I never saw him again. Since that day, and in the days that followed, besides a bruise he had left me all his emptiness, because he had stolen (almost) all my inner wealth.

In his apathy he is probably convinced that he stole my dreams and that I will never be the same as before. In one thing he was right: I am no longer the same as before. I am stronger and more determined. And about the dreams he stole from me... well, he took the wrong ones.

Reflection: this story shows that the manipulator, after the first moment of love and unconditional acceptance (he knows how to read people well), often passes from psychological violence to physical violence, without exception.

The story of Adele, 37 years

I was 19 when I met M.

M., 16 years older than me, was not handsome but very charismatic, confident, and generous. He was a hard worker, economically secure and never missed an opportunity to boast about it... He covered me with compliments and gifts. He made me feel like a princess; there were countless social occasions during which I was even embarrassed by the way he praised me, with his friends and family. I felt lucky.

I was economically independent; I had my job.

When our dating became serious (almost immediately), I started to frequent his house, spending the weekends at his place.

I started shopping and cooking for him. It seemed like a nice way to make him understand how much I loved him, that I wanted to take care of him.

I couldn't afford to reciprocate his expensive gifts with something as expensive. I slowly gave him myself as a gift. I felt safe.

In 2004 we got married. Since he had a job of his own, he wanted the regime of division of property, to which I was not opposed. I found a job near his house (he lived 60 km from Vicenza). After only six months we were expecting our first child. The joy of that period was immense.

Towards the end of the pregnancy something started to change. He assiduously reiterated to me that I looked more and more like a "bull". That I was getting fat as shit and that he was beginning not to be physically attracted to me anymore.

I was impressed, sincerely, but I elaborated this admission of his to make sure that I didn't let myself go, that he cared about me... After the birth of F. I tried to lose the weight I had gained during my pregnancy, but this was due to breastfeeding and the long days I spent alone in the house, he didn't even mention going down, on the contrary.

A few days before my return to work, after the leave for pregnancy, my owners informed me that they would put me in mobility, to put in my place the wife of the owner, who had replaced me during the period of leave.

The moral thrashing was terrible.

My husband reassured me by telling me that maybe it was a good thing, because I could take care of him and the baby full time.

I intensified my work in the office by my husband, who until then "used" a girl who only came on call. I cooked for clients who came to make samples and managed the house. My husband gave me 800 euros per month for expenses.

With the birth of my second child, I started to feel suffocated by that routine and the constraints that the amount of 800 euros gave me, with two small children and the recurring dinners. I tried to talk to him about it, making him aware of my difficulties. His answer was: "What's the difference? If I give you 100 you spend 100 and if I give you 1000 you spend 1000! You are not able to handle the money!". I clearly felt his lack of trust and made it mine. He was right! In fact, I never advanced one euro at the end of the month.

So, I decided to put myself back in the game from a business point of view.

I was on probation with a fixed-term company for three months, which then hired me indefinitely. I was happy. L., the little one, had been placed in the nursery, F. was going to kindergarten, I was working, and I still continued the activities of before (M.'s office, dinners for clients...).

My husband never participated in family life, he never picked up the children from school, he never took them to the pediatrician or had an ice cream. He was too busy with his work. The salary that I received was entirely used for the payment of the nursery fees, but despite that I would not have given up that job for anything in the world!!!

A couple of years later, however, the economic crisis forced the owners to transfer the accounting management of the company to their accountant and put me into mobility. I was trapped.

My husband reassured me by telling me that I didn't need to work, because he would have taken care of it, so clearly, I wasn't able to keep a job... He was right...again!!!! In fact, nothing told me otherwise...in effect.

I was locked up at home. I had no friends. Our only acquaintances were limited to a few dinners with his friends a couple of times a year. On weekends instead we would leave with the motorhome to indulge his passion for motocross which, after his work, was his priority. I gave up.

I decided to believe that the only thing I was able to do was to "serve" my family. The world did not esteem me, I did not deserve it. If he hadn't been there, I probably wouldn't have done anything.

Thus, began what I only now recognize as the dismantling of my ego. "Superb, selfish, ignorant and excessive, ugly, vulgar, fat, disgusting...". This is what my husband repeated to me almost daily. I could not propose that we go out for a pizza. I was told that it was easy for me that I did not know where the money came from. If I bought a T-shirt from the Chinese, I would be recriminated that my hands were pierced, and I would be mocked. He started accusing me of having a lover, he would check my phone and my car mileage. He never missed an opportunity to tell me that without him I was nobody.

A couple of years ago, his sexual attitude changed. He used to look at pornographic sites before coming to bed and demanded that we had sexual intercourse every night. He didn't make love. He was aggressive and overbearing. If I didn't respond as he wanted, he would call me frigid or accuse me of having someone else. In the evening, when I heard him going up the stairs, I started to feel sick, I felt nauseous.

I was deeply convinced that the problem was mine. I, who should have rejoiced in the desire that my husband had for me after eleven years of marriage. I felt guilty and I interpreted that violence as a small price to pay to have the wonderful life that he told me I was doing but that I, ungrateful, did not recognize.

I had a hard time surviving and adapting to that situation.

One morning, while the children were at school, I suddenly felt my heartbeat faster and a strong feeling of fear that evolved in a few seconds into the feeling that I was going to die. I was convinced it was a heart attack! Like in the movies, I saw my life pass me by.

In the evening I talked to my husband about what had happened in the morning and his answer was: "Let's hope you finally decide to get treatment! Did you finally realize that you are completely out of it???".

I felt like I was living in a nightmare. But I had also convinced myself that it was me who was having problems.

I asked myself: "Why do I feel so bad if instead the world told me that I was so lucky?".

There was no doubt: my husband was right again!!!! I am ungrateful, selfish, and greedy. I do not know how to enjoy my fortunes. I felt truly guilty.

One fine day I discovered by chance that my husband was cheating on me. He didn't have a mistress, he had many, he even frequented prostitutes.

It was a slap in the face! It was one of those blows that make you wake up with an uproar.

It took me a few days to understand what was going on. It was like lifting a very heavy woollen blanket, impregnated with dust, which hides a very shiny, almost new mechanism that had been stationary for years...

It was all fake, I had canceled myself for something that did not exist.

But why had I allowed him to treat me like that? What had happened? Where was I and what was I doing? Why?

I felt like I was suffocating, I didn't understand where to go. The people around me were telling me to forgive them, that it wasn't something so serious... For a moment I even believed them!

Then I decided to go to therapy. I needed to find myself before making any decisions. I felt that I was not there!

After seven months since that fateful day, it has not yet happened once again that I have regretted the choice of separating. It is a difficult path. He doesn't want to, he doesn't resign himself to having lost his power over me, he is making me sweat this path, making it difficult and often getting in my way. These difficulties, however, I realize only now, are rehabilitating me to life. Never have I felt that I am not alone! A circle has formed around me, a protective net that I would have never even imagined. People I had excluded from my life have returned, running towards me with open arms.

I had the courage to ask for help. They answered my request en masse. "I am not alone! I will never be alone!".

Reflection: from this story emerges the importance of "asking for help", recognizing one's own suffering. This is the first step toward salvation!

The story of Lisa

I am Lisa, I am thirty-eight years old and I have a story to tell. I met Giulio on Christmas Eve. Despite some behaviors that, given the lack of knowledge, I attributed more to a certain insecurity, he seemed caring and, according to friends and family, in love for the first time in his life. Our story began and after a month and a half he unexpectedly gave me a record. I was happy about it. I was in love. Despite this, it began immediately unexplainable behavior on his part for a person who calls himself in love.

Why didn't you believe me? Why continue and nagging questions? Because phrases such as "To me it seems strange that you are returning from Florence, to me it seems strange that you are single? He nagged me about my exes, he wanted continuous explanations, he made jealousy scenes. At the same time, however, he never called me, he was never present because he gave priority to his friends and family. He was very immature and above all he believed everyone but me and told me that if everyone says something, then it is true. I was always the fool who didn't understand. He never missed an opportunity to humiliate me in front of everyone. He told me that he would have wanted me to work with him, to keep me under his control, which then happened. I only got a lot of messages on the phone saying how he was jealous of his parents and friends because everyone liked me, that I was his and that from the very first moment who had seen me had thought "This is mine"?

I gave daily continuous explanations, even if already given and not due, about everything. After a few weeks he asked me the same thing. I told him that I seemed to have already explained why, but he told me not to remember. Was he pretending about everything or was he not aware of anything? He told me that I was crazy, because I got nervous in front of so many explanations given and given a million times, he stroked my head like a dog and told me to be quiet, laughing. And in the meantime, I had to justify myself continuously, exhausted, so as not to be believed a priori about my personal affairs and my past. He would slander and slander me unjustly with his parents (and not only), who believed him. He questioned everything. I, very direct and sincere, I who still believe in truth and loyalty, I who believe that to love and choose a person means to believe and give priority and trust I found myself without reason after a few weeks in front of all this.

He began to defame and offend a former acquaintance of his. He called her crazy, sick, and anorexic. He slandered this girl even with his colleagues who did not know her. I did not understand the purpose. That ring he had given me ended up being immediately criticized by friends and his sister-in-law. And I still didn't know any of them. He felt badly about the criticism he had received. Instead of selecting and evaluating people, he found himself prey to the judgment of others and asked me for advice. I had been defined by unknown people as "the first one who passes by and takes a ring". I told him very calmly that in his place I would go to those people to explain quietly that perhaps it was better not to judge his feelings and respect them. They were offending him before me, since they were his friends and not mine yet. If they had been true friends, they would not have done so. That boy had only fallen in love with me. He accused me of wanting to ruin his relationships with family and friends. He accused me of not letting me get along well with his friends; instead, both with them and with his family, once they met me, I was comfortable, I loved them and tried to deepen relationships with a view to a future together. He slandered me to keep me under his control and isolate me and in doing so the others moved away from me. He blamed me, that I had to pass over the insults they did to me (which turned out to be the result of his slander to keep me away and isolated; to maintain his image he damaged my relationships with his family, always very attentive and kind to me). But he was always with his finger pointed at me. It was more comfortable for his image and his goals. He always defined himself and felt like a victim. He creates and combines everything by himself, but it is always the fault of others or mine. His best friend told me that he was always a difficult guy, but I tried to confront him. I am good and I tried in my heart to help a person that I perceived as disturbed and who manipulated reality or the meaning of my requests, ruining a relationship just to make everything revolve around him, as he wanted. He immediately told me that he would never leave his home. He proposed me all the precarious solutions for a future and linked only to his world, because he told me that he was afraid. He had no plans, never. He could not realize them, always blaming others with malice.

In the following months I found myself the victim of a careful and devious work of physical and psychological isolation on his part. When I called him in the evening after work, he answered me badly saying that I was disturbing him because he was at the bar with friends or at a friend's house drinking and playing cards. I was extremely sick because, if I had known, I would not have disturbed anyone, I said to myself. Besides the fact that I did not understand where the disturbance was. I was in love and excited to hear my boyfriend, but my chatter about how my day had gone bored him, he told me. With him we never talked about anything. If I didn't call him, however, when he wanted me to, it was criticism and jealousy. He controlled everything for me. I asked him to tell me where he was going or if he had any programs during his free time, to know how to adjust and organize. But my request was translated into defamation, into metastasis between friends and family because, according to him, I was jealous, and he couldn't even stop at the bar or go out with friends. It was all tampered with and absurd. With every observation or request I made to improve the relationship - at the beginning we didn't know each other, and he had never had an affair, except for a very brief acquaintance years before made up of a few meetings and that's all - he accused me of talking so much for nothing and that I was crazy and sick. I was trying to explain to him that only dialogue leads to knowledge and understanding of misunderstandings.

He told me that his father offended me.

He started telling me that he preferred to leave me rather than lose others. He started telling me that his parents and family said I was crazy and that they couldn't wait for us to break up. He told me that my sister-in-law talked badly about me and so did what I thought was a dear friend of mine. She told me with a lot of aggressiveness and malice, but above all with satisfaction. How to say, do you see that everyone thinks like me? You are the crazy one. I always felt under observation and wrong. I turned to a psychologist, now convinced that I was wrong. I was sick, I didn't understand, I was crying and the more I cried the more he felt strong. I was trapped in his canvas.

His mother, seeing me suffering, asked me for explanations. She then told me to leave him, because he deserved to be alone, having always been like that since he was a child. She said it seemed strange to her that he had found someone and that if he didn't get what he wanted, he would clench his fists and everything would turn red and if things didn't go the way he wanted, if everything wasn't under his control, he would scream. One day he grabbed me by the neck for it too, but I ended up not being believed. I was always moving with respect and sincerity, he was maneuvering everyone, he was telling lies and changing reality at will just to discredit me. A conscious computer. When I was away from him, he alternated moments of sweetness, attention, and excuses to take me back under his control and organized a weekend together. I did not understand why those same people he mentioned to me were so nice to me when we went out. But I believed him, because my value of love was to believe who I had chosen, otherwise nothing would have made sense.

But slowly, after so many verbal aggressions and unpleasant facts in this regard, tormented to see so much kindness even from her parents, I decided to address these people directly, asking them why. The latter were astonished and denied it. So much so that the parents asked him in front of me why he did so, and his father scolded him. He reacted laughing, saying he had done something stupid and he didn't even apologize. As if nothing had happened, he started sending me flowers and telling me that I was unique, to convince me to stay with him.

In addition, he had obsessions with other women. He told me openly that all the other women were more beautiful and better than me. Inside a supermarket he followed a girl, in the office another one, and the evenings with his friends were evenings in which he kept on making remarks to me because I had a skirt too short or he expressed jealousies if someone paid attention to me. He would stare at the other girls for evenings. I'm not talking about a normal comment or appreciation, but obsessive and abnormal behaviors aimed at staring at shoes, feet and back of all girls on any occasion. He was always dissatisfied and insecure of what he already had in his hands and had been chosen by him. He was a gentleman with me opening the door to get out of a club just to turn around and wink at the girl sitting next to the door. Clearly, he defined me with everyone crazy and jealous, as he did with his ex. For me it was just lack of respect and a humiliating and absurd attitude.

We went hiking in the mountains, a passion that I had transmitted to him, and his only dialogue was to talk badly about his sister-in-law or girlfriends of friends because they did not allow his brother or friends to come with us. He always wanted someone with him. He didn't know how to do anything on his own. His phrases were "Even my such friend says that his girlfriend...etc.". He invented or exploited other people's situations that did not concern him or compared me to girls who had nothing to do with me, just to achieve his goal, to keep me under his control and continue to do what he wanted to discredit me to others.

The fact that he and I were alone was a source of discomfort for him. I asked him some explanations and, seeing how he treated me, I also asked him why he did not leave me... His answer was that the problem was not me but that he felt alone in two. It was his problem. But if we were in a crowded room, he told me that if he was not next to me, he felt observed, but with me he felt safe. He needs to be in a group and to be accepted by everyone and have everyone's approval. He told me that if we lived together and I stayed home sick, he would go out with friends or family, because if he stayed home with me, he wouldn't let me get sick. He told me that if one night his friends asked him to go to a nightclub, he could never refuse, otherwise the others would think he is stupid and dominated by a woman.

He wouldn't even give up a dinner with friends, he would go even if he was sick. If some girlfriend of friends couldn't go out, they would change the date so that we could all be together, but if I couldn't, he wouldn't propose a date change, but he would say: "I'm going alone". When I asked him to visit me, he was always tired, but for his friends he was always there. There was no comparison, I did not exist. I was the one to show how and when he wanted me. And his guilt work on me was exhausting. It was my fault; I was sick, and everyone believed it. I went to dinners and no one looked me in the face anymore; even my famous friend answered me very badly in front of everyone. And he said to me: "Do you see that you're taking it too hard? You see things that aren't there, you're crazy". And he knew very well what he was doing behind my back. We were going out with his friends, and I was the only one who lived far away. He wouldn't pick me up or take me home, never, not even once. He would take everything for granted, he would make me run at night, during dinner he would get drunk and offend me and the next day, even if he remembered what happened, he would laugh, pretend nothing happened and tell me that I was taking it too much and that life is one. He would disappear for days. I found out that he had signed up for a trip or a walk with others or that he had gone to parties without inviting me because he had decided that I would say no. And when I gave him the remark, he told me that I was sick and shit. And so, he told everyone. He told me that I was selfish because I went to the beautician. It was the only thing I allowed myself. I didn't go out anymore, I neglected my old friendships, I didn't go to the gym anymore and I lost weight from suffering. I spent my time demonstrating, destroying myself, to a person that I was sincere, good. I had lost my sunshine. In front of all this he was having fun. If I was at home sick, he would not come to see me. He wrote to me during working hours, after that he no longer existed and told me that I had to learn and that if I learned, I deserved a gift. And then he would come with a bracelet or flowers or something. Always everything inexpensive. I never asked for a gift, for me a flower picked from the ground is more precious than anything. But he emphasized that he didn't want to spend too much for me because it wasn't worth it.

He neither travels nor goes on vacation. To go on vacation, I would organize everything as he wanted, a maniac of order and perfection, and I would book where he and I were least likely to be alone. For his personal gain on vacation, he was affectionate. The nightmare started again as soon as he got off the plane on his return. I knew that he would start his game again. And so, he did. He excluded me from everything after making a thousand promises. He has no plans in life and does not want to take responsibility. In fact, he never went to live alone, not even before he met me. He blamed me for wanting serious projects and teased me about important and cheap projects saying that I would never make it. I also suffered financial losses because he said things or made promises that he didn't keep and told me that I had misunderstood. I made it, believing it and with people next to me who believe in me. And working hard and with loyalty. With silence, and not with the discord as he did.

I always worried about being sincere, I showed him that even if I received invitations and various courtships from guys I knew before him, I refused them. But I always had to prove it. If I said goodbye to someone I met, he was jealous, if I didn't, according to him I hid something. He was paranoid about everything. My correctness was a weakness for him, and he worked with his manipulation. The more I wanted to reassure him, the more he invented and told lies. He took the phone out of my hands in front of everyone, even though I was writing to my mother. The more sincere I was, the stronger he felt. I confided to him especially important things about my life and the next day I found myself that everyone knew them. I got angry, I lived it as a lack of respect as it is, but the result was receiving accusations, because he hadn't done anything wrong and I was the one having problems. I never confided anything to him again, explaining that he always slandered me as a liar. Could I have trusted him?

He started slandering me in the office where I worked and fortunately some intelligent people told me about it, recognizing in him many sick attitudes.

He used to follow me during my work to see who I was with, I found him by surprise during the day behind me. He would slam doors and imagine relationships that I didn't have just because I was online at the same time with a colleague for pure fatality. When I told him that he was like a dagger in my back, he laughed. The more I explained, the more he pretended not to understand, the more I cried and explained the more he amused himself by making the situation worse with his wickedness, not realizing that in the end he hurt me, but he did it mostly to himself. He was asking around his colleagues about the double personality alluding to me. Crazy. I was crying depressed in bed, instead of kicking him, and the more I didn't get out of bed the more he mocked me and was absent.

He lives on the image he created that of the good guy who helps everyone, always smiling. In front is this, behind is a monster that people do not know. Not all of them, fortunately. He is available to everyone, except to show himself what he is not. Those same people are his victims. He gives priority to his image and uses others to maintain an image, he lives on frivolous and false relationships. Those are enough for him. When he has ground to walk on, created with his falsehood, he is fine. He uses friends and colleagues and discredits his partner because it prevents him from being selfish and narcissistic. To isolate me he has slandered all the people who have been close to me. I also had a beautiful relationship with male colleagues, but it was not good. One by one he took them all away from me. The important thing was to hurt me, isolate me and make everyone believe that I was a bad person. Losing all contact with everyone. If those people knew...

With colleagues and friends, it was all thoughtful, but it was a different person. He told me strictly personal facts about his family and his sister-in-law to make them look bad and to keep them away. When I left him, he asked me what he had to do for me to stay with him. I asked him to see a psychologist, but he told me that it was money wasted and that he didn't need it. I told him to tell everyone how he had behaved, and he made me believe it, but I found out it wasn't true. He slandered me every day and isolated me more and more. He went out with me, but he didn't tell anyone. I wasn't in love anymore, I didn't like him anymore, he was gone into disgrace. He did not listen to me, but he believed the others. And so, he lost me, destroyed me, and made me sick. But he also hurt himself. A person cannot do that... To say that he loves you and that he wants to spend his life with you, the life that he called hell with others.

Clearly this relationship had no other destiny than the end. I left this boy two years ago. I have been suffering violence, stalking and slander for two years. He contacted my ex-boyfriend and his ex-boyfriend. He wants to return with me at all costs. I found out that the ex-had already reported him to the Carabinieri for stalking while he was with me and the first thing, he told me describing him was that "He exploits your weaknesses and is disturbed, he is a persecutor and bad". I found myself in the same game. He was contacting me and her at the same time with the same invitations and requests. The problem? That he always presents himself behaving beautifully with others, because that's where his underlying problem comes from. He is not ashamed of anything. He has been called several times by lawyers to put an end to the stalking, not to get to the complaint, but he did not stop. They are under his continuous control. And some people, even in front of an order of the removal judge, still have the courage and ignorance not to believe. They too are victims of his power and slander. It was nice to laugh in the face of my suffering, my slimming, my anxiety, and illness.

Reflection: from this true story emerges, in addition to the evident emotional manipulation and psychological violence protracted on the victim to the point of making her sick, the ability to lie that these disturbed personalities have, to the point of deceiving more people, going from executioners to victims.

A very painful thing is then the lack of solidarity and loneliness in which the victim lives, without anyone who fully understands her pain.

Finally, from these stories you can understand how the victim of manipulation struggles to break away from his persecutor for fear of being alone.

I remind readers of an old and wise popular saying: "Better alone than badly accompanied".

Chapter 5

The levels of severity of emotional dependence

The term "severity" indicates a set of characteristics that cause concern in relation to the possible or current harmful effects to which a relationship characterized by emotional dependence can lead, i.e., the level of danger to the welfare of the victim of this condition.

Assessing how serious emotional dependence can be must necessarily be done on several levels, as it is impossible to anchor this assessment to some standardized tests or structured interviews. In emotional dependence, as well as in other forms of dependence, particular attention should be paid to three specific areas that determine this problematic condition: the subject (the emotional dependent), the object of the dependency (i.e., the partner with whom a relational emotional and dependency bond is established) and the environment/context in which the relationship survives.

Motivation to change

A first important level to consider, to assess the severity of emotional dependence, is the motivational one. It is important to establish initially the level of motivation of the patient to understand if the patient is willing to change his behavior in the couple relationship or if he is still considering having a problem or not. The "famous" wheel of change of Prochaska and DiClemente (1980) can help us. This wheel (see image above) shows how a person can be in one of the different stages of change and how these are influenced by environmental, psychological, social factors of various kinds.

The first stage is that of precontemplation: in this "phase" we are dealing with an emotional employee who has no awareness of his or her condition and the risks associated with it. It may happen that someone notices that there is something wrong, you realize the problem, but the affected person minimizes or even denies the discomfort he is experiencing. In this phase it is necessary to work to build a minimum of motivation to change, making the subject more aware of the problem (the slices of salami are removed from their eyes!!!).

In the contemplation phase the person begins to feel a minimum of willingness to change, he realizes some negativity he is experiencing and oscillates ambivalently between one extreme (I am not well in this situation!) and the other (all in all I am well in this situation!). In this case you must work hard to build and strengthen this "embryo" of motivation for change.

In the phase of determination, the person has finally reached the decision to want to change the situation he is living. He begins to see that the positive aspects of the relationship with the partner are not so beneficial, the negative aspects become dominant. The person is therefore more willing to listen to others (friends, family, specialists) and their suggestions. Even in this phase there can still be moments of failure and the person can "retrace his steps". It is therefore necessary to work incisively on short-term goals and strategies to achieve them, to facilitate the transition to the next phase.

The moment of the action establishes a sort of virtual boundary in which the person actively interrupts the behaviors that keep the addiction on its feet and is "physically" oriented to the action, implementing strategies and useful advice to better cope with the dysfunctional relationship.

Maintenance phase: once the desired results are achieved, it is important to maintain them. It is therefore essential to reinforce in every possible way the positive changes that have been implemented, aware however that there is the possibility of reinvigorating oneself in a relationship where there is dependence (relapse). Being aware of this adds the right amount of attention that helps us to prevent behaviors that put at risk our well-being again.

Comorbidity

Another level to consider is that of comorbidity, i.e., the fact that the patient also suffers, in addition to emotional dependence, from psychological problems (depression, anxiety, other forms of addiction) or personality disorders that can aggravate the situational picture and thus complicate the possibility of being helped. As already mentioned, the personality disorder, for example, strongly binds the person to the partner because the fear of abandonment and loneliness can be so unbearable that he prefers to remain in an uncomfortable situation (but that you know perfectly and, in some ways, reassures). The picture is therefore aggravated when the emotional dependence is associated with these disorders, requiring greater efforts to "break" the vicious circle of malaise and negativity.

The characteristics of the partner

Speaking of couple, it is necessary to consider the characteristics of the partner, a fundamental element that helps to keep the relational dependence alive. The considerations made for the victim are therefore valid: if the partner suffers from personality disorder (narcissist) or a form of addiction (e.g., alcohol), the situational picture worsens considerably. In this case, we are aware that the efforts made with the "victim" of the relationship to break the dysfunctional behavior can be countered strongly by the attitudes of the partner.

If the situation is characterized by episodes of serious physical violence, psychological violence, and skillful manipulation by the partner, then we are faced with a condition that, in the most extreme cases, requires articulated, multidisciplinary, and even timely interventions (if the risk for the victim is particularly high). In this regard, it is worth pointing out that there are associations ("Volere è Potere" for example is one of these) and Women's and / or Anti-Violence Counters in many Italian municipalities that are organized to deal with situations of this type.

The socio-economic condition

Another condition that can facilitate or complicate the process of change is the socio-economic condition. We cannot deny that financial possibilities constitute a not insignificant aid factor. Let's think of "normal" couples, who come to a separation simply because of conflict or because of the extinction of the feeling of love: the lack of money sometimes "forces" (where there is no support from the family of origin) to a forced cohabitation, because there is no economic possibility of finding another house to rent. And when there are children within the couple, the level of complexity can become even worse.

Second part

THE 5 PRACTICAL MOVES

First step

How to get rid of the dance of manipulation

There is much talk of physical violence, but all too often we forget the seriousness of psychological violence, defined as "murder of the soul". It is therefore a devious crime and often not even recognized by the victim. Men, women, and children are indiscriminately involved in emotional manipulation.

The intensity gradient may vary, but in all cases, it is harmful to mental and physical health. This form of violence is intricately linked to emotional dependence because the dominant partner uses it to have power over the victim.

Returning to the patterns set out in the introduction, both the dominant and the dominated have deeply rooted the pattern of "inadequacy", acquired in childhood because of lack of affection, gratification, and satisfaction of basic needs. The former adopts the style of overcompensation to mask his weakness, while the latter uses surrender because he surrenders to his lack of "perceived" value, choosing partners that lower his self-esteem and thus confirming that he is not worth it.

There are typical behaviors that demonstrate this subtle form of violence and which I will list below with some explanatory examples.

- The dominant partner, verbally and non-verbally, emits behaviors of continuous and subtle humiliation of the partner. For example, he always makes the other one feel inferior, unsuitable for him, unable to handle normal life situations. Such devaluation can also be made in front of others with "half sentences" such as: "If I were able to cook, it would be a different music" or "But how did you dress today, my dear?".

- It also emits continuous devaluations of the victim, often made in a playful manner. For example, he can say: "When I chose you, I really had to be 'out of my mind'", accompanying the sentence with a smile, or with the implication of the series: "Fortunate is he or she who has a capable partner at work!", when the husband or wife has difficulties at work.

- The manifest guilt is a constant because the dominator always attributes responsibility to the other, making him feel guilty. Remember that guilt is a lethal weapon that takes away energy and lowers the self-esteem of the person who feels it. Even if he admits guilt, the dominator adds that he was put in the situation by the other, otherwise he would never have behaved like that.

 - He often leverages the weaknesses of the other or his ideals of love, friendship and loyalty with the so-called moral blackmail that is the basis of the sense of guilt and inadequacy, with phrases like: "You who talk about ideals and values treat me this way!

- Excessive jealousy is a constant because the manipulator gradually isolates the victim from friends and family, to have absolute dominion over the other person. The emotional dependence, in fact, manifests itself with the progressive isolation of the victim who, living in function of the other, also loses interest in the activities she once liked. The dominator, through the moral blackmail of the series "Prefer your family to me, the gym to our relationship", weaves the spider web in which little by little you are imprisoned.

- Another way of domination is to play the part of the victim to be pitied. Remember that the victim is often an extremely dangerous aggressor who is not always recognized. The typical phrase is: "Leave me alone, with everything I have done for you!".

- The lack of clear communication is a constant because it allows you to "turn the tables at will". Let us remember that clarity is the basis of healthy relationships. To encourage mental confusion in the victim, the dominator often gives vague answers to precise questions or changes the subject during a conversation, always with the aim of confusing the other to the point of deforming or interpreting the truth according to one's own benefit. This subtle manipulation confuses the victim to such an extent that he becomes increasingly succubus. To this is often added ignoring the requests of the other, with phrases like: "You didn't speak clearly, and I didn't understand your needs", "If I had been more precise, I would have done what you asked".

- The dominator also and often creates discord to isolate the victim from friends, acquaintances and family with phrases like: "Your friend hit on me, didn't you notice?" or "Your brother makes you feel inferior because he has a degree, and you don't. Is it possible that you didn't get it?".

- The manipulator knows how to lie without shame or guilt, because he uses all means to dominate the other and make him more and more dependent.

- Dulcis in fundo, he is also envious of the success and talents of the other, so he tends to underestimate him because he is in competition with him.

What are the effects of emotional manipulation on the victim?

First, the loss of self-esteem and, worse, of identity, with mental confusion and sense of entrapment, anxiety, and panic disorders, eating disorders, depression at increasingly severe levels and development of addictions, primarily alcohol. Sometimes the victim may trigger a sense of rebellion but being impulsive, it can lead to further guilt and entrapment. In many cases, when the victim rebels, the dominator may also resort to physical violence to maintain the emotional dependence of the other.

At this point you will wonder what to do in such cases. If possible, close the relationship firmly (see "Second Step"). If this is not possible, avoid the trap of clarification, of wanting the manipulator to reason, because you risk getting even more confused and feeling even more trapped.

The personalities most likely to dominate are narcissists and psychopaths. We spend two words to identify them.

Narcissists

Since this is not a treatise on psychology, I will list some characteristics of narcissistic personality disorder. First, the person who is affected by it needs constant attention and admiration, to the point of being jealous of their children when the lighthouse is not focused on her; she constantly wants to dominate in a relationship, becoming aggressive if she can't; she completely lacks "empathy" and is unable to put herself in the shoes of others. The result is selfishness and the claim that others should do everything to meet her expectations. She is arrogant and conceited; she has fantasies of success, power, and ideal love; she blames others and manipulates them to achieve the satisfaction of her needs.

Sometimes this disorder manifests itself openly (overt) with a sense of grandiosity, called in common parlance as typical of the "bloated balloon". In other cases, it manifests itself through physical or psychological illness, often imaginary or exaggerated, as well as alcoholism, to have power over others. And this mode, called covert, is more difficult to recognize.

It is right to point out that narcissistic personality disorder has a genetic basis on which educational dynamics are triggered within the family of origin. Unfortunately, this disorder is exceedingly difficult to treat even with the help of psychiatrists and psychotherapists. These individuals, unable to question themselves, constantly repeat the same mistakes, ruining relationships, falling into depression, and remaining alone in old age.

Psychopaths

Psychopaths have a genetic deficit in the limbic area of our brain, so they are not able to feel emotions other than anger. For this reason, they report to feel a sense of emptiness. They also have a deficit in the frontal area of the brain, so they are not able to control themselves and are slaves to the impulse. For this reason, they can become violent and fall into forms of sexual promiscuity or serious addiction to alcohol, drugs, substances, and gambling.

They recognize themselves because they have a great sense of importance, they lie without shame and guilt, they don't feel emotions even if they pretend to feel them (in fact they are born actors), they tend to make a parasitic kind of life by joining people who exploit also economically, they are very skilled manipulators, they always need stimuli not to fall into boredom and to overcome the sense of inner emptiness. Their ability to lie can lead them to have a dual personality. Psychopathic benefactors on the one hand and perverts on the other are not rare, just to give an example. Psychopathy is incurable.

Because of the sense of inner emptiness, they can go as far as suicide.

Does emotional dependence only occur with violent, narcissistic, or psychopathic people?

It seems to me to mention two types of relationships that create emotional dependence and that often are mistaken for true love: love of a symbiotic and caring kind.

Unfortunately, the lack of education in healthy love produces false beliefs in people that condition their lives by creating suffering. The most widespread and celebrated in many love songs is: "I can't live without you... you are my world...", so that people understand that love is an addiction, because if there is no you, I am nobody, I have no value. From this comes the conviction that without the other the person cannot achieve his happiness. Thus, is born the dependent attachment, in which partners, friends or family do everything together, maybe even work together and deny themselves moments of autonomy because otherwise they feel guilty.

In love, such a close bond, too close, inevitably leads to boredom, closure towards the outside and friendships, so important in life at all ages, and the lack of stimuli, so that the relationship flattens and little by little sexual attraction is lost. An example of a symbiotic couple that comes to mind is the one in which, after years of isolation from the world locked in the bubble of the relationship "two hearts and a hut", she fell in love with another and he attempted suicide because, accustomed to living in symbiosis with her, he had lost his identity. The paradox of love in fact reads: "I am autonomous, and I am good with me, but I prefer to be with you". At this point, the relationship becomes a choice, no longer a need.

With friends, the same thing happens. When a friendship is too close, it is destined to end, because the other is taken for granted and the relationship flattens out. The excessive closeness, then, leads to the inevitable quarrel, which ruins even the best of friendships.

In parent-children relationships, addiction is lethal. The parent does not often let go of the child, reproaching him for everything he has done for him or making him feel guilty if he starts a life of his own. Other times it is the child who, in order not to take responsibility for his or her life, remains attached to the parents until his or her or the parent's death, as many cases I have had experience of in my work as a psychotherapist demonstrate.

Our culture, unfortunately, does not favor autonomy, because the child who remains attached to his parents is considered a good son. Let's not forget, however, that in any emotional relationship it is good to have the right distance: neither too close nor too far away, always maintaining one's autonomy and independence.

Another type of love that is addictive in the couple is the caregiving one, in which a partner with the syndrome of the Red Cross if it is a woman or the Good Samaritan if it is a man becomes the parent of the other. This type of bond also develops addiction, because the "son/daughter" does not take a step without consulting the other, to whom he tells everything. This bond is also destined to end over time, because sooner or later the physical attraction comes to an end (how do you want a parent or a child?) and the couple remains bound by a sexless relationship or one of the two, often the child, finds the lover.

Second step

How to end the relationship with a violent manipulator and how to defend yourself in case of need

If possible, consult a psychotherapist for information, support, and advice on how to act before terminating the relationship. Your partner may also be involved if you accept this. This will promote resilience and greater effectiveness in the termination of the relationship.

Another recommendation is not to engage in any parallel relationship if you are tied to a manipulator. His reaction, should he discover you, will certainly not be peaceful. Reading the facts of the news, it is clear in many cases that this can even lead to murder.

I always advise my patients or during classes not to start other relationships while you are busy, even if you are unhappy. It is a question of fairness. Zen masters say that you cannot fill a glass if it is still full.

As already mentioned, for the most predisposed personalities there is a natural transition from psychological violence and isolation to physical violence towards the weaker side, with the peak in case of abandonment. The author, therefore, evolves his role from manipulator to abuser, going so far as to become a stalker or murderer as, unfortunately, the facts of the news show.

The ways of contrast must therefore go in the direction of defense and protection of the potential victim and the collection of evidence.

It is essential not to deny the problem out of fear, shame, and guilt, because often, since no one wants to consider themselves victims, they tend not to recognize themselves in danger underestimating the risk and favoring the author. In addition, talking about it with an expert as soon as possible would help to identify the level of danger, to predict or imagine the next steps for an effective intervention.

Seeking an experienced psychotherapist in this field facilitates awareness, supports the self-esteem and courage of the victim in countering the persecutory acts of the abuser or stalker and, if the latter accepts it, in helping him/her to overcome abandonment. Statistics show that more and more perpetrators, especially men, if properly informed, become aware of their state and accept the help offered.

There is, however, a set of rules that it is useful to know and apply, to implement a defense to avoid possible serious consequences in case of unpredictable excesses put in place by the abuser. First, it is necessary to be firm in saying "NO" when you decide to break the relationship: once and clearly. Any further effort to convince will be read as a reaction and will be a reinforcement, because considered attention. This applies both to everything that happens in presence and indirectly. For example, the receipt of a gift should be politely rejected. Another important thing is not to get compassionate by accepting the last appointment, which for some women was fatal. Let's remember the news story in which the Veronese lawyer at the last dinner killed his former partner.

Then all those "common sense" measures should be taken, normally considered but which, unfortunately, many times the victim, due to the state of prostration in which he is, is unable to apply. Then implement simple prudent behavior, avoiding routine habits and isolated places. For example, if you go to have breakfast in the usual bar, it is appropriate to change the place or avoid going to work always going the same way.

It is also useful to buy a second cell phone, for two important purposes: the first, to have a spare device if the abuser manages to take possession or destroy the device normally used, as well as to make calls in case of emergency; the second purpose is to have a new number with which to communicate if on the first one the persecutor sends messages and makes calls at all hours. The fact of changing number without keeping the first one active means for the stalker one more reason to continue the persecution with greater strength and would motivate him to have a direct contact with the victim.

It is also essential to keep all calls and messages received, possibly without reading them, because it would increase the fear and discomfort of the victim. On calls, if it is the home phone, it is advisable to answer them by hanging up immediately so that, if necessary, the received calls can be highlighted on the phone records.

For cell phones, this is different, as "missed calls" are tracked. However, the practice of "answer and hang up" would also be useful in this case if you do not expect to have to involve a forensic expert to demonstrate the contacts (only the rings are not traced) and in case you receive calls with an anonymous number.

Equipping yourself with a tape recorder to crystallize the conversations if you meet the persecutor in the usual places frequented or near the home or workplace, to use what you have acquired in case of complaint. The same function can be performed by the cell phone, if compatible, with which you could also produce photos or videos.

If you think you are being followed by the abuser, it is best not to go either to your home or to relatives or friends, but to the nearest police/carabinieri office. The same authorities should be informed by telephone to ask for help using the emergency numbers (the call is recorded) when you are unable to reach the barracks quickly or the danger is imminent, for example the pursuer tries to block the road.

All the activity mentioned in part, aimed at the defense and the collection of evidence, should be integrated with a diary in which are recorded all telephone contacts, visits and actions taken by the harasser to always have control over the victim, to increase his need for attention and his emotions.

The victim should be noted and documented (photos and possible testimonies) even if they are not causally related or demonstrable now, for example the violation of the mailbox or damage to the car, as they could be traced back to the persecutor.

For greater protection, if there is the possibility and for the purposes of the request for intervention of the bodies in charge (police and judiciary), it is useful a private investigator who, following a regular assignment, could monitor the movements of the abuser to document them with a dual purpose: to ensure greater safety of the victim and to show them in court as evidence in favor. For example, a GPS installed on the car will be stable when and how many times the persecutor has physically approached our person, without our knowledge.

It is also useful to know how to make a complaint. First, it becomes fundamental to know how to discern what is supposed to be from what is, i.e., to report the facts and not the impressions that, in most cases, may constitute grounds for heated contradictions against the victim during the criminal proceedings that will be undertaken, with consequent second victimization. Thus, the complaint and the way in which it is collected and recorded assumes importance. It is from this, in fact, that the police and the magistrate must obtain all the elements necessary to reconstruct the hypothesis of the crimes that can be committed.

The victim, however, can contribute effectively by making up as much as possible for the deficient situations that may be encountered in the formalization of the act.

First, it is a good idea to report with a detailed list of the facts considered harmful that have been suffered, specifying chronologically and in summary for each of them, supplemented by time, place, name of any witnesses and their contact details, any photographic or audio material.

If known, the name of the author, any personal data, telephone numbers and vehicles in use. About sms and phone calls received, it is useful to produce the details (day, time and, when possible, telephone number of origin), as well as the transcription of the texts of the messages and a summary of the content of the relevant communications; the same applies to emails. If "de visu" contacts have occurred, regardless of whether they are accidental or not, a precise list should also be drawn up for these, specifying the circumstances and details.

If damage to property has occurred, if you have not requested the intervention of the police, it is good to photograph the damage, starting from the general to the, and show the photos.

Accompany everything with any medical or veterinary reports if animals are involved. If a psychological damage or discomfort has been recognized, you can show the specialist documentation. In these cases, certificates relating to episodes far away in time but attributable to the current author should also be exhibited.

In the case of receipt of mail or paper messages deemed to be related to the situation, these should be attached and the way they were found should be explained. Eventual delivered objects, if not cumbersome or dangerous, must be exhibited during the verbalization. In a different case it is good at least to photograph them.

As far as possible, always contact the same police body, perhaps the one close to your place of residence, to avoid the dispersion of the acts and jeopardize the speed of action.

It is recommended to be decisive, whatever the path you want to take.

Third step

Practical self-esteem exercises (the welfare grid and affirmative rights)

From some research a good self-esteem is the basis for a life free from addictions of all kinds.

Unfortunately, in our culture both religious, where you must be good and not to sin in order not to offend God (but being imperfect how do you do it?), and social, where to be worthy of value you must be young, thin, rich, happy (but not too much, otherwise they envy you), competent (but not too much, otherwise they bully you), having self-esteem is not easy.

And let's not forget that from two years of our life we are instructed to grasp the negative. If at school you behave well and study, you have done your duty. If you make mistakes, save those who can. The first confession is a list of sins that the child is often forced to invent, the mass media (newspapers and the news) do nothing but bombard us with negative messages of deaths, attacks, murders, robberies and so on. The black key scheme prevents us from grasping the positive that life offers us and pushes many people to see only their own defects, those of others and what is wrong in their lives.

In the light of all this, people start with a basic low self-esteem that, as has been said before, leads to two similar attitudes but with opposite manifestations: underestimation, in which the other is always better in every field, and overestimation, in which the individual reacts to low self-esteem proving to be "strong, good, perfect, never wrong", then making himself hateful.

We now come to the clues of low self-esteem and the advice to raise it, in other words, the antidotes.

Clues of low self-esteem

Rigorous self-criticism

First, rigorous self-criticism, accompanied by an inner dialogue that can be compared to medieval penances. As soon as the person is afraid or makes a mistake, the negative internal dialogue begins with phrases such as: "I made a mistake as always... I'm stupid... I'm not worth it", immediately followed by the second clue, the sense of guilt for not being able to make a mistake.

be successful, not to be perfect. I call this attitude "horror of error" that, we must put it in our heads, is part of our life and is fundamental for our improvement, for our growth. Some readers may think: "Yes, okay, but if you make a mistake, others will blame you for your mistake". You are right, but in the meantime learn to change your inner dialogue and to respond to others: "Wrong is human, no one is perfect, you learn by making mistakes.

How to get rid of it?

Beyond that, I would like to teach you a simple exercise to change your negative inner dialogue. If your best friend was wrong or afraid, what would you tell him/her? Surely you would be kind to him, perhaps by saying: "Everyone makes mistakes... come on, you'll see that you'll succeed". We should use the same encouraging words with ourselves. Think that positive inner dialogue is the first step to building good and healthy self-esteem.

For this small change it is necessary to train every day in a constant way.

Fear of judgment

Another sign of low self-esteem is the fear of other people's judgment: "What will others think of me?". How many times have we asked ourselves this tragic question! Tragic for what reason?

Because the fear of being judged can lead to immobility or to follow the rules to be accepted, renouncing our personality. In the end, we risk making a life that is not ours. I am thinking of how many young people smoke, drink, or take drugs to be accepted by the group, how many adults, for fear of making mistakes, have done a job that they did not like and that did not give satisfaction, how many people have remained together unhappily for this reason. The paradox is that whatever we do, it will not exempt us from other people's criticism and the most frustrating thing will be that we have given up on ourselves in order not to be approved anyway.

Being undecided

Indecision is a direct consequence of the previous clues. The person who is afraid of making mistakes, who is not encouraged, who is afraid of other people's judgment will surely be indecisive.

Never asking for help

If things do not go well, it is important not to fall into the other clue of low self-esteem: never ask for help or ask too much. Many people give up at the slightest mistake, without trying to ask for help because they consider it a sign of weakness. Recognizing that you have a problem is an act of strength that triggers change and is a demonstration of courage.

On the other hand, there are people who ask for help for every nonsense and never really put themselves to the test, because they are afraid of making mistakes or of judgment which, as we have seen, is another sign of low self-esteem.

Ultimately, an old saying goes: "In life it is not important never to fall, but to get up after every fall".

Perfectionism and dutifulness

Perfectionism and dutifulness are intricately linked. As I have already said, our culture is steeped in perfectionism, of the series: "You have to be perfect and therefore you have a duty to...". Just think how many times we repeat the word "I must" in our inner dialogue: "I have to phone that customer... I must make this turnover... I have to do the shopping etc.". The person fills himself with duties to keep abreast of the times, to the point of renouncing rest, recreation, and dialogue with others, which are necessary in our lives.

Keeping everything inside

The lack of emotional communication is another sign of low self-esteem, but we will talk about it in the next chapter.

Anassertivity

Complacency and aggressiveness towards others damage not only self-esteem, but also relationships. This topic will be discussed in the next chapters.

Sadness

Sadness is one of the consequences of low self-esteem. After all, a person who has a negative internal dialogue is afraid of the judgment of others, feels guilty, is unable to communicate effectively, can certainly not be serene and satisfied with himself, his life, and relationships with others.

The rights of the person

To consolidate self-esteem, it is good to know what the rights of the person are, because others can manipulate us to act as they want us to and have power in the relationship. Have you ever felt emptied after a discussion in which you have not come up with anything?

This happens in relationships where you are manipulated because the other has sucked the energy out of you. We have talked about psychological violence, but we have to say that these power strategies are quite common in interpersonal relationships because they are learned in the family of origin. It is important to become aware of them, to avoid suffering them or putting them into action unconsciously, otherwise you risk ruining relationships over time and extinguish even the greatest passions.

Starting from the assumption that not even siblings feel the same way, even though they have had the same family, we can imagine how impossible it is not to live in situations of conflict with others.

The most used power strategies are essentially three:

- The first is implemented through guilt, blaming the other when he does not give in to our needs. All of us can report situations in which the partner has blamed us or in which we have done so. Of the three is the most lethal strategy, because many are inclined to feel this feeling because of the inhuman social and religious norms I have already mentioned.

- The second is expressed through a sense of disapproval when our behavior or ideas do not conform to those of parents, friends, partners. It can be manifest. Silence is one of the worst strategies and can last for days, until one is forced to give in, becoming the unsustainable situation of a couple or family.

- The third one is carried out with a sense of ignorance when the person who wants to have power there accuses of not knowing, of not being up to the task. This strategy is widespread in working relationships, but also in couples when the other is more educated or pretends to be so.

Here then is listed the affirmative rights that, through awareness, offer us a way out of this yoke.

The affirmative rights

1.We all have the right to be respected by others, regardless of age, gender, sexual orientation, economic status, level of education.

Unfortunately, in the workplace or at school this often does not happen. Even in a couple's relationships it can happen that one partner manipulates the other, making him feel inferior because he is less well-off, less educated, or younger. If this happens, we learn to defend ourselves, saying: "Even if I am less rich, educated, different or younger than you, I have the right to be respected, as I do with you".

2.We all have the right to have needs and desires that must be considered as important as those of others.

In emotional relationships, many stifles their needs to satisfy those of others, particularly in dependent relationships. Instead, we must understand that we too have needs that need to be satisfied for the duration of the relationship, even if others manipulate us with disapproval. So, it would be appropriate to respond: "I understand that our needs are different. We must therefore find a solution that suits us both".

3.We all have the right to feel all kinds of feelings and to express them in a respectful way to others.

Remember that emotions and feelings cannot be judged, unlike behavior. If the partner should manipulate us by making us feel guilty or disapproving, we can answer firmly: "Everyone has the right to feel feelings and emotions that must be accepted and controlled by both parties. For example, if you feel dislike towards your partner's parents, you can show them respect but you cannot and must not necessarily love them to please the other, otherwise you would fall into falsehood.

4.We all have the right to decide whether to meet the expectations of others or to act according to our own needs and desires, without harming the rights of others.

It is important to distinguish between right and desire. If my partner is sick, if he is sick, he has the right not to be abandoned by me, but if he wants to go to a disco and I am tired, I am not obliged to meet his expectations. If he tends to make me feel guilty or sulk, I can tell him firmly: "Excuse me, but I don't feel like dancing with you tonight".

5.We all have the right to have our own opinions and to express them correctly to others.

The manipulative partner may blame when the other's ideas are not like his own, manipulating with the implicit rule: "If you love me, you must think like me". As I expressed in the clues of low self-esteem (the fear of judgment), the person can answer: "I accept your point of view, but I do not share it" without feeling guilty, angry, or hurt, otherwise you fall into the trap of manipulation.

6.We have the right to change our mind if circumstances or our life experiences favor it, without being blamed by others.

This manipulation also happens for small things, let alone when the person decides to end a friendship or a relationship. Many people will have happened to accept an invitation that has been cancelled due to health problems or unforeseen circumstances. You can certainly also say that in some cases the other has done or at least tried to make you feel guilty. Let alone when you decide to end a relationship. When two people get together, they do it to get to know each other and to understand if they are good together and if there is an affinity. Few people are aware of the four alternatives of a relationship: the first is that the two people are happy and that the relationship is consolidated (everyone hopes so); the second, that people leave each other (which is rare); the third, that they stay together unhappily for them and their children (which happens frequently, of the series: "and lived unhappy and unhappy); the fourth, that one suffers because one is left by the other, who realizes that he is not happy, that he no longer loves and then trouble begins, because our expectation is that love will last forever, especially if married. This is the main cause of many situations of psychological and, alas, physical violence.

7.We all have the right to decide if we want to provide justification to others for our behavior, without disrespecting them.

The education received prompts many to provide explanations for a certain behavior or for choices made. We are not required to give them. For example, if a friend or acquaintance asks us why we did not show up for a certain period, making us feel guilty, we are not required to justify ourselves, but we can say that we could not meet him. If we decide, and it is not mandatory, we can explain why.

8.We all have the right to judge our own behavior and what is right or wrong for us.

I remember the case of an old friend who criticized me, manipulating me with disapproval, because at my no longer green age I wanted to take a new course of study. I told him that everyone is free to decide what can make him feel good and that, if he didn't think like me, I respected his idea.

Another example is that of Valeria, who decided to finish her university course after a period of suspension. When Marco, her partner, asked her for explanations, she replied in a kind but decisive way that it was her need and that it would certainly not have damaged their love and their relationship, on the contrary it would have strengthened it.

9.We all have the right to ask for explanations or information for what we do not know, without being considered ignorant.

For example, Carla, during a dinner with friends, asked for explanations on a subject. When her husband Eugenio told her that she couldn't not know that fact,

manipulating her with a sense of ignorance, she replied that it is normal not to know all the human knowledge and therefore it is correct to ask for explanations for what you do not know.

10.We all have the right to decide whether to take care of ourselves and solve the problems of others, without being blamed or feeling guilty.

The manipulator very often uses guilt to have power over others. As Jesus Christ said, we must love others as we love ourselves. There is a law of balance between our own needs and those of others. As a result, we do not always have the energy to take care of others. In this case, we must not prevent ourselves from saying no. There is in fact "compassion syndrome", which affects people who are too sensitive and altruistic, leading them to depression. Instead, it is good to allow yourself some space for yourself, in case you really want to help your neighbor.

11.We all have the right to be paid for the work we do. Asking for the bill is an act of justice that many people do not have the courage to do, as on the other hand in our day too many people have no qualms about not paying.

The three moments of the couple

In order not to fall into the trap of emotional dependence, it is important to remember that the two partners, even if in pairs, need moments of autonomy, where they can devote themselves to their hobbies, friends, activities. There is a beautiful poem by K. Gibran, taken from the book The Prophet, that we should all remember.

The second moment of the couple is that of sharing, because in life it is important to do things together, to share friendships, activities, and pastimes with the children, otherwise you would end up getting lost.

The third moment, no less important, is being together as a couple without children, to live understanding, intimacy, sexuality. Many relationships have ended because this important moment has been missed. They are lost in routine, in the lack of intimate sharing and their relationship has resulted in boredom and silence, which become fertile ground for betrayal.

The grid of well-being

It is closely related to what has been said so far. In my book: La coppia che scoppia che scoppia, edizioni Il Punto d'Incontro, I talked about this and I report it now:

... Every person, married or in couple, should, at least monthly, devote attention to the following aspects of life:

- hobbies, which need not necessarily be those of the partner. Being in love does not mean being the same and thinking the same way - each person is unique and must have moments of autonomy.

- personal growth, which should last a lifetime, trying to look inside, to find the time to do so, trying to improve the character sides that make you and others suffer.

- reading: you can't just read the Gazzetta dello Sport or stick in front of the TV. Reading helps to broaden your vision of life, to learn new things, to grow, to become more interesting because you have more things to say.

- friends, who are important in every moment of life. It's not right to remember them only when he or she has planted you; if they send you to hell at that point, do an examination of conscience. Many consider their partner as their only confidant, but certain things cannot be said to their partner: you would make them suffer. ... Certain confidences are better to make real friends, who have the right detachment to listen.

- physical activity, especially in contact with nature, is good for the body and spirit, keeps you in shape, doesn't make you feel sick, and whatever else...

- time for themselves, to relax, to sleep, to run... Many people, after the birth of their children, cancel themselves and, if they dedicate some free time, feel guilty. In fact, for them good partners and effective parents it is important to find time for themselves.

Fourth step

Practical exercises to accept, manage and communicate your emotions

If you feel positive emotions, no problem. But when you experience negative moods, you find it hard to accept them and you blame yourself. But, since we all have a positive and a negative part, it would be essential to accept them in any case. After all, how would we know we are happy if we had not experienced sadness? Men have no problem showing anger, but they hardly show anxiety, fear, sadness, jealousy for cultural and social factors: "man must be strong! For this reason, they live less than women, who instead can freely express their emotions. Up to a certain point, of course. Why are we talking about emotions? The reason is simple: in our culture, emotions succumb to reason, to the list of facts and things that happened, unless they are negative. Would you like an example? The husband comes home from work and the wife asks him how it went. Often the answer is: "As usual". Wouldn't it be better to answer: "I felt unmotivated and bored"? So, of the 120 emotions we should experience every day

we notice few and usually, alas, negative, so our relationships become impoverished.

Having said that, I would like to talk to you about the emotions that do the most damage to health and relationships: anger, anxiety, sadness, jealousy, and envy.

Anger

What is anger?

Good question. Most people think that an angry person is bad and therefore judges, blames others and of course themselves when they get angry. In fact, anger is the manifestation of grief. Why do we get angry?

The reason is that we are angry. So, it would be better to tell the person that we are disappointed, rather than raise our voice.

So why do we get angry?

Because someone has disappointed our expectations, has treated us unfairly, has not considered us, has criticized us, or judged us, has stood us up, has told falsehoods about us, has tried to cheat us, betrayed us, usurped our role, etc. And from our stomach/intestine starts an energy, the so-called "embolus", which makes us see "red", which makes us shake our hands and upsets us like a river in flood.

How does anger express itself?

There are individuals who, in order not to create conflict, for fear of the aggressiveness of others, for fear of making them suffer, keep silent and consent or rather, cash in. What are the consequences of this way of behaving? That a little at a time, if we do not react, the other will take advantage of us until, in extreme cases, we are humiliated. Added to this are physical disturbances because, since anger is a form of energy, if we don't express it, we burst into it. And here are the headaches and gastrointestinal disorders serious.

By dint of taking blows, we bend under the weight of the pressure suffered.

Then there is the category of aggressive people who assert their rights, opinions, needs by force, shouting, offending, saying heavy things. Result? Even if they may have been right, they go over to the wrong side and do not reach the hoped-for goal with their communication, on the contrary, two possibilities will occur: either the other one will collect but brood resentment and sooner or later - remember - he will make you pay for it, or he will get angry in turn and then save who can!

To this is added the physical malaise of the aggressive, who with his explosion produces adrenaline "a gogo" and after the age of fifty is at risk of heart attack, perhaps after having ruined his relationships and feeling guilty.

The classic attitude of the aggressive is one of rigid posture and fiery gaze.

Then there are individuals who are complacent with some and aggressive with others (usually those who love them, like family members) and others who, after a long time immediately, with the classic drop that overflows the pot explode and say everything they have not said for years and then really save who can!

But then what can you do?

Here are some useful tips. First, when you feel anger and you see red, you must imagine yourself in front of a hypothetical traffic light for RED that invites you to stop and take a break. We can say: "Let's talk about it later, otherwise we risk entering into conflict".

During the break, it is good to try to relax by running, jumping rope, chopping wood, taking a walk in the park, listening to music, etc. Once you feel calmer, you can meet the other person and simply say: "When you behave or talk to me like this, I feel uncomfortable, I feel sick, so we have to find a solution that is good for both of us".

At that point we try to mediate between our needs and those of the other.

But then we should never get angry?

I point out that it is better to try to make the other understand our point of view with kindness. But if after twice that we explain it to him, he does not understand, then it is legitimate to get angry, because maybe that person was used to this way by her parents when she was a child and then "yes".

feels at home" only with aggressiveness.

The resentment

It is lawful and normal to get angry for a wrong at once, but it is harmful for ourselves to feel resentment, because we unfortunately enter a dead end. The grudge is an aggravation in the time of anger, accompanied by a continuous brooding over the wrongs suffered. The mind elaborates in negative the situation and the person who has committed it, adding nuances, projections, generalizations, paranoia, etc. To get out of it, it is necessary to be able to observe consciously, that is, without blaming and blaming oneself. Until the grudge turns into forgiveness, we do not get out of the trap of suffering, a sign that we are inexorably hostage to the games of our mind. So, let's come to the next step and see how this is possible.

Forgiveness

Forgiveness is above all a healing from the past and a going beyond. One forgives the person who has wronged us when one understands that he or she acted in a profound condition of unconsciousness. Forgiveness must come from the heart when you understand that the person who has wronged us is perhaps a victim of himself, of inadequate mental patterns that, however, determine his unhappiness.

The true forgiveness then, having at its base the understanding, moves our being in the dimension of love, instead of making us stay in that of resentment and hatred.

We can practice the art of forgiveness "by degrees of difficulty", that is, starting from small daily episodes, for example, the person who wants at all costs to put the car in our place in the parking lot when we arrived earlier; we must think that maybe she has her own problems or is a victim of her mental limitations, perhaps due to sad childhood experiences in which she did not receive the love, understanding and security she needed.

The forgiveness of we are then a fundamental step. Because others are our mirror, the moment we forgive them, we automatically forgive ourselves for our mistakes.

What if we cannot forgive? Then it is important to go further, without dragging the weight of the past like balls to the foot.

Anxiety

Among the emotions considered negative and that create discomfort we find anxiety. Like all the others, it has a level of intensity. Comparing it to a scale from zero to ten, where zero corresponds to tranquility and ten to panic, we speak of annoying anxiety from seven to ten.

Like all emotions, it has its adaptive function, because it indicates that there is a danger and activates the muscles when it is associated with fear of an obstacle, often unfortunately imaginary.

How does it manifest itself?

First, with accelerated breathing, with muscular tension ("My stomach closes, I tighten my jaws and grit my teeth, my muscles are tense, I blush and sweat"). A bit of anxiety is normal, and it is right that there is. Think of a person who does an examination too relaxed: he would not give his best performance.

When it rises to 10, you may experience a panic attack that gives the feeling of dying. But it's just a feeling. To my patients, when they are out of breath, they feel faint and have tachycardia, I say: "Think of a soldier at war... Panic doesn't make him die, it takes much more than that!".

What does it come from?

Anxiety has various implications. One of the first of these is linked to anger, because both the aggressive that explodes and the passive that takes in have states of anxiety, because emotions are linked.

Like all states of mind, anxiety is linked to the thoughts that the person formulates. The aggressive thinks: "I am afraid of being attacked or overwhelmed, I have to defend myself, so I attack first". The complacent thinks: "Careful, you are about to be attacked... you must behave at your best... otherwise it's trouble".

Then there is the anxiety linked to the fear of making mistakes, of failing, of making a bad impression, of the judgment of others, of guilt and sexual performance.

Why is that?

Have you ever heard of "inhuman social norms"? We have already talked about it, but it is good to repeat it. You must be handsome and young, otherwise you run like the products, you must be thin, happy but not too much otherwise they envy you, competent but not too much otherwise they bully you, up to the point of "seeking apprentice with experience". Who wouldn't get anxiety?

Then there is the anxiety related to the future, typical of those who do not live the present, do not even remember what he ate for lunch because he already thinks about the after. Who thinks too much about the future, maybe in negative, lives strong states of anxiety: "I will remain alone...? I will not find the right person... I'm going to fail the exam... My partner will leave me... I will remain without money...". And whoever has the most, of catastrophes!!!

How can this be solved?

By increasing confidence in oneself and in others, first and foremost.

The aggressive one must learn to speak with kindness, and he will achieve much more. The violent have never had a good ending, it's enough to read the story.

Those who are too good must learn to think that they too are good, that they have their rights and that it is enough to express them clearly.

Those who experience anxiety because of fear of judgment must reread the clues of low self-esteem contained in this book in Chapter 3.

Those who live fear of the future learn to live the "here and now", as our right hemisphere teaches us. If I think of something negative about the past, I feel anxiety. If I think of the same thing in the future, what do I feel? Anxiety. So, our right hemisphere works in the present. We begin to taste the moment.

"But what does this psychologist say?" will some of you think. "You have to think about the past and the future!". "Of course," I answer you, "but also and above all the present because it is now that I live. What happened before no longer exists and what will happen tomorrow has yet to happen"? And then, if we are more optimistic, we will have less anxiety and we will live better, making beautiful things happen, as the scholars of the brain have shown with the phenomenon of the prophecy that is self-fulfilling.

We smile more, we are kinder to others and to ourselves in our inner dialogue.

And for those who suffer from panic? Let's learn to breathe more deeply, up to the belly: two or three deep breaths in the morning, at noon and in the evening, also doing gentle physical activity, because we don't have to compete with anyone. What if someone tells us that we made a mistake? We answer that no one is perfect.

Sadness

Another emotion demonized by our culture is sadness. If a person is sad, rather than feeling inadequate and marginalized by the company that already has enough problems, or blamed "because there are always people who are worse off than you", he pretends nothing, he is stuffed with antidepressants, isolates himself and is even worse off.

What to do?

Start to accept the sadness, answering to those who criticize us that "laughter abounds in the mouth of fools", as the ancient Romans used to say.

Men, blamed from birth with the typical phrases: "Don't cry, you look like a sissy", repress the sadness maybe by drinking, throwing themselves on women, at work or sticking to the computer or TV to distract themselves. They don't even recognize that they are sad and maybe they go to the doctor or psychologist saying: "I have a knot in my throat, I have a weight on my heart...". Here, these are the somatic manifestations of sadness.

As with all emotions, there is a level of intensity. If 10 represents the depression that makes you stay in bed, that does not show anything good in life or even makes you think that you are not worth living, you should go to a doctor and a psychologist.

Depression at level 6/7 is called mood deflection, called "dismount" in Veneto. At this level you notice little, if not from clues such as poor motivation, restless or disturbed sleep, poor appetite, but above all a decrease in sexual desire. These are the unequivocal signs that there is a drop in mood, a wake-up call that something is wrong in your life.

What causes depression?

As I said before, it is a sign that something is wrong. It can be guilt of the past, disappointed expectations, regrets of things not done or not said, anger never expressed, needs never satisfied, nostalgia for the times that were and that cannot return...

The important thing is to understand why and what gradual changes to make in your life.

Do thoughts also influence this case?

Of course, they do. The depressed person tends to formulate negative thoughts such as: "It's my fault, I was wrong, I'm worth nothing, he took advantage of me... [we remember that too much good is often disappointed], the future will not reserve anything good... [catastrophic thought], it's all my fault... [personalization], everything goes wrong [negative filter]".

The thought determines sadness, with a curved posture under the weight of life, because sadness, linked to anger and anxiety, takes away energy and the person is often tired.

Then there is the sadness determined by obsessive negative thoughts: "I will be punished...I must wash myself often...otherwise I will die...I am contaminated...I will kill my son...I am insane". He who has this kind of inner dialogue cannot be happy and, as research has shown, fearing that he will become insane, falls into depression.

How is it possible that a person has such negative and repetitive thoughts?

It is possible, unfortunately, and this stems from feelings of guilt towards parents who have not been able to meet the most important needs of the child: affection, gratification, understanding, security, dialogue and listening. The child, who is not able to make a correct analysis of reality (i.e., thinking: "My parents have problems... they are not happy... they are stressed"), blames himself thinking he is worth nothing and feels anger generated by suffering, which he feels guilty about. Becoming an adult, he self-punishes himself through obsessive thoughts or ritualistic behaviors, such as counting continuously, washing for several hours, checking light, gas, etc., until his life becomes hell.

What to do?

As soon as you realize that you are sick, that you are sad too often, that you cry for nothing, that you feel a knot in your throat or a weight on your heart (men, listen to me!), that you lose your sexual desire (women, it is for you!), instead of pretending nothing, ask yourself what is wrong in your life. Try to make small changes for yourself, to do the things and activities you like. Give yourself some space for yourself without feeling guilty if the house is in a mess if the children are in a mess with grandparents. You too are entitled to the famous "airtime" like the prisoners.

If you realize that you don't want to live anymore, run to the doctor, have a psychotherapist follow you and put yourself in the head that who goes there is normal, not crazy, and that, if anything, it is these last ones who don't want to know about it (the crazy ones, therefore).

Try to change your thoughts from negative and irrational to positive and rational. For example, if you think it is always your fault, make a proper analysis of the situation to see if others also had to take responsibility.

If you want to avoid being disappointed, speak clearly about your needs without thinking that the other person should understand them. He will not understand them even if you tell him, let alone if you keep quiet.

Try to think positively and, if your husband is late, do not think that he is dead, but that he has had a setback.

Again, speak even after years of things never said and never clarified, you will remove a burden. And if the other does not understand or gets angry? That's his problem, at least you will feel lighter, without remorse and regret.

Finally, you begin to keep a daily diary or at least, if you really don't have the time or the desire, weekly, to write down the positive things done or happened, otherwise our mind, which suffers a continuous bombardment of negative things and facts (guy kills his wife and shoots himself or tries but prefers to turn himself in or escape... terrorism... always new diseases), focuses only on the negative, neglecting the positive that there is always in life. Whoever thinks positive smiles more often, lives longer, is happier and makes others happier.

I conclude with a quote: "If you have a problem and you can solve it, why do you worry? If you can't solve it, why do you worry?". For me it was a panacea and I hope it is for you too.

Jealousy

Here is another emotion demonized by men: jealousy considered a sign of weakness. When a man is jealous, he says that it is not true, that it is a matter of principle, while the woman accepts it and admits it more easily.

In love it is normal to be jealous, so we should not be ashamed to try it. I point out, however, that this feeling must be contained, because when it exceeds certain levels it becomes pathological. Let us think of jealousy between brothers, which is often condemned by phrases such as: "You are bad when you are jealous of your sister... It is wrong to be jealous...". We cannot judge or condemn feelings and emotions; we can judge actions. People who condemn jealousy refuse to accept it within themselves. For example, a parent, to do good for his child, should say to him: "It is normal for you to be jealous of your brother, as long as you behave well with him".

Jealousy can refer to objects, people, their activity, their ideas, their feelings. I repeat that the important thing is to contain it, otherwise you will become a slave to your morbid attachments. It will become a prison that we build by ourselves causing unspeakable suffering.

Sometimes it can be a parent to be jealous of his son, if father, or his daughter, if mother. This is because the father tends to identify with the firstborn male son and, usually, if he has an activity hardly gives up, because he does not want to lose what he has built or is afraid that the child

may turn out to be better than him. Add to this the Oedipus complex, of which no one has ever explained anything to us, so that the male son from three to six/seven years old tends to fall in love with his mother and to be jealous of his father, as if he were a rival. This lays the foundation for the crisis of the father/son relationship described above.

The mother can also be jealous of her daughter, especially about her physical appearance or professional achievement, if she was forced to give it up. For the female also applies the speech of falling in love for the father from three to six/seven years old which, as for the male, sometimes puts the mother/daughter relationship in crisis.

Then there is the jealousy between mother-in-law and daughter-in-law, which is another sore point in relationships between partners. It is no coincidence that we speak of "mother-in-law's milk", i.e., a liquor that has an extremely high alcohol content, or "mother-in-law's pillow" to indicate a fat plant full of thorns.

Here too it is normal and depends on overcoming the Oedipus complex. One should never exaggerate because excess leads to suffering.

The jealousy that harbors misfortune is between partners. It is often mistaken for true love: "How much he loves me, he is so jealous! Excessive jealousy is pathological and is based on possession, not love. So, the person who is too jealous, who says: "You can't laugh or talk to someone else, because even your laughter must be mine" denotes great insecurity, low self-esteem or, worse, a projection. Let me explain better: the jealous person sees in the other his infidelity.

The jealousy, then, pushes to control or inquisitorial behaviors (follow the partner, check his cell phone, emails, ask him questions to verify) that, if initially lower the level of anxiety, then involve in an obsessive ritual:

On a somatic level, it manifests itself with a pain in the heart area, a "sword in the heart", as quoted in a Little Tony song.

I always recommend people to doubt too jealous partners because, in case of a break-up, they could become stalkers. These people are often too jealous already during the relationship and do not accept that their partner is someone else's. Sometimes this is determined by the way the breakup happened.

Another form of jealousy is also the jealousy between friends or girlfriends, which manifests itself primarily when one of them finds a girl or a boyfriend, who becomes the object of anger.

What to do then?

First, accept it within us, because this passage allows us to accept the others' and control it.

Then, do not let yourself be caught up in the ritual of control, which foments doubt and jealousy.

Finally, write down your progress in your diary, after you have set yourself the goal of controlling this painful feeling.

Envy

One of the feelings that the person just does not accept to feel is envy, depicted by an old woman with snake-like hair, because it makes you feel resentment, with liver pains. It's no coincidence that there is the saying "to eat your liver".

In fact, envy is also a human sentiment. If we want something so much that is denied to us and our friend, partner, brother, son, neighbor gets it, it is normal to feel envy. The important thing is to accept it and find a solution to inner pain.

I report my experience. I too felt envy towards a friend of mine who had recently given birth to a daughter, when I was told that I could not have children. For twenty days I fought against this bad feeling, until I found a solution, a way out. I decided to write (books are like surrogates of children we bring into the world), to leave a trace of me. Only after I had worked out the solution, I went peacefully to visit my friend.

When envy manifests itself between partners, we talk about competitive love. Let's explain better: a person chooses a partner for his or her qualities that, indirectly, honor and make her proud. Later, however, envy begins to creep up, so if the person does not become aware of it or does not accept it, it can lead to serious damage in the union. For more information, watch the film The War of the Roses.

Envy is extraordinarily strong in friendships, where people hang out and, above all, confront each other. This also happens between sisters and brothers, because if we don't confront each other, the others do, with phrases like: "How beautiful is your sister...how good is your brother...". I would add if people would learn to keep quiet! Parents often do it, innocently, to stimulate a child to be as good as the other.

Then there are cases of envy among relatives, including between parents/children, and when it leads to hatred, it is a truly pathological thing. There is a saying that reads: "Snake relatives, knife brothers".

Again, it all depends on intensity and duration.

Envy can be positive and negative.

Envy is negative when the person tries to take revenge on the best or most deserving one. One way is gossip. If you envy someone, you try to damage them by spreading rumors that ruin them as a person or at work. I don't think it's a good idea to dwell on it...everyone knows gossip, unfortunately.

Negative envy lasts over time and makes those who try it eat gall. Moreover, if the recipient is aware of it, it also creates problems for those who suffer it, especially if the envious uses devious systems to take revenge. Think of Mozart and Salieri: one is dead, the other has ruined his life.

Envy towards a classmate leads to bullying, towards a colleague leads to bullying, towards a partner to psychological and physical violence.

Negative envy brings suffering to all parties involved. It is based on a generalized comparison: "The person is better than me". I explain myself better. The human being tends to compare himself with others to establish his value and to overcome his limits. It would be more correct to say to oneself: "The person is better than me in this aspect, in this field". This statement would have a different impact on our self-esteem and would create less envy.

The comparison leads, in some cases, to the inferiority complex, which can have two consequences. The first leads the person to underestimate himself, to consider himself wrong, causing anxiety, depression or, in the most serious cases, alcoholism and various addictions. The second causes the superiority complex, in which the person, feeling inferior, tries to retaliate against others, with aggressiveness and arrogance, as unfortunately many historical figures have shown.

How to get out of it and make the envy positive?

First, remembering that each one of us is unique and has its own value, that each one of us has merits and defects, that the important thing is to value what we have and constantly try to improve our defects, not to be better but happier.

Then, as I said before, change the mental scheme by comparing only one aspect and if anything, use the other as a model to improve.

Finally, the best thing is to confront yourself. What have I improved about myself compared to the past?

Fifth step

The effective way of communication to express needs, necessities, to mediate and defend against the bullying of others

In interpersonal relationships, people oscillate between two opposite behaviors: passivity or complacency, typical of dominated people, and aggressiveness, which distinguishes dominators.

Starting from the assumption that not even siblings have the same opinions, let alone what happens in couple and interpersonal relationships: having different ideas, conflicts will inevitably be created and there will be one person who wants to win over the other.

The complacent or dependent person does not express his opinions or needs, for fear of being abandoned, of breaking relationships or making the other person suffer. They are often afraid to unleash the other's aggression. She may even go so far as to express criticism, but she does so in an uncritical way, so her communication is ineffective. In both cases it is as if it conveys the implicit message: "You can take advantage of me". The person with this style of communication gets to the point, with the "classic drop that overflows the pot", to explode and become aggressive, except then to feel guilty and return to please the other.

The aggressive, manipulative/dominant person, instead, expresses his ideas and needs in the wrong way. In fact, he shouts, attacks, blames, and humiliates the interlocutor, because he is afraid of being overwhelmed and losing control of the relationship. With her explosion, she often creates the submission of the other, who, however, harbors resentment and resentment, which irreparably damage relationships over time.

The passive-aggressive person, a strategy also adopted by dominators, is the one who imposes himself by indirect means, making the other feel guilty or wrong or pretending to joke but meanwhile annihilating him.

The effective communicative style, called assertiveness, is to assert one's rights, opinions and needs in a clear, sincere, direct, and respectful way of the other. We talked about this in the previous chapter, about anger.

Assertive communication is based on correct and rational beliefs which I list below:

- We strengthen our self-respect when we defend our rights in a firm and responsible manner, making ourselves known to others.

 - when we act in a way that never offends anyone, in the long run this does not benefit us or others.

- when we express our ideas and needs, we allow others to get to know us and relate to us appropriately, changing their behavior for the health of the relationship.

- If we sacrifice too much, we end up giving others the opportunity to take advantage of us.

We must remember that it is one thing the rights of others, which must be respected, and another are their wishes and expectations: it is not right to harm the rights of others, but it is unfair to go against oneself to satisfy their wishes.

The techniques of effective communication

Expressing praise

Everyone, including us, needs to be rewarded, but the way you do it is crucial. It is important to describe the behavior we appreciate in each other. Let's take an example. If I say to one person: "I really like your drawings", my praise will be appreciated, while if I say: "You are an exceptional drawer", it can be interpreted as a mockery, except for narcissists.

How to receive praise

When you receive a compliment, it is always good to welcome it, otherwise the embarrassment is mutual. It is not necessary to reciprocate immediately, otherwise you lose spontaneity and can be experienced by the other as a forcing.

The sentences of appreciation are healthy for any kind of relationship. Unfortunately, the manipulator does not compliment the victim to exert more power on her, on the contrary, as we said, he often devalues her to lower her self-esteem and increase her addiction.

How to express one's desires

The person who lives in a state of emotional dependence struggles to express his or her desires and, if he or she does, is often not taken into consideration. But it is also true that many people are the victim of the wrong idea that I call "mind reading" and which takes the form of the phrase: "If he loved me, would understand what I need". The others sometimes do not satisfy our desires even if we tell them, much less if we keep quiet!

It is also important to use the messages in the first person and not to refer to generic standards. A correct message is this: "I would like you to listen to me when I speak" and not "polite people listen", because the first sentence is descriptive, the second evaluative and can cause irritation in the interlocutor. Only by giving short, clear, and precise messages can we avoid manipulation.

How to protect yourself from the bullying of others

As we have already explained, the manipulative, dominant person tends to be overbearing, imposing his point of view on us, or pushing us to behave as he would like. For example, the dominant wife tells her husband: "Let's go to the party with my friends", the husband replies that he doesn't feel like it because he has to get up early the next day. Then, the wife presses on, saying that they wouldn't be late. The desperate husband says he also has a headache. The final line of the other is: "Don't worry, I have a phenomenal pill".

This example shows that the more we provide excuses, the more we give the bullies the chance to impose their will on us.

In such cases it is good to adopt the defense technique called broken disc, that is, always repeat the sentence that expresses clearly and directly what we want. To return to the previous example, the husband could say to his wife: "Darling, I'm sorry, but I don't feel like coming to the party. I will gladly come another time".

This assertive behavior allows us to insist on our legitimate desires without falling into manipulative verbal traps by the interlocutor and without being diverted from our personal goal.

Another defensive technique is "clouding", which assumes that in established relationships one person expects a certain behavior from the other; for example, he knows that by making a certain kind of speech the other will get angry. In this case, clouding means doing the opposite of what the other person expects, so stay calm.

Another defensive technique is selective attention, which consists of paying attention only to the speeches that make us feel good, ignoring others who are made to manipulate us or make us feel bad. A patient of mine, victim of a manipulative husband, learned to say: "I respect your point of view" and to change the subject when he insulted her. In this case, she applied the double technique: clouding and selective attention, disarming him.

Finally, the technique of separating the cues allows you to defend yourself from the bullying of the other while keeping the topic of conversation firmly. Many times, during a discussion, the dominant and overbearing person, who always wants to be right, tries to take the conversation elsewhere to divert attention from the problem that was being addressed, to be right. In this case it is useful to say: "We are talking about this problem. When we will have found a solution, we will talk about this one".

All these techniques are based on respect for oneself and the other.

Negotiate

Starting from the assumption, as I have already written, that not even siblings having the same family have the same opinions and needs, we must accept that we will never find a person who thinks like us and who has the same needs as us. Consequently, conflict is inevitable, but solutions must be found that suit both parties in conflict. Negotiation is in fact called "the win/win technique" because there is no one to win the power struggle.

If the dominating partner or those who try to manipulate us by making us feel guilty, disapproving and making us feel ignorant, we must react by saying strongly: "We have different ideas, and it is normal that this is the case. Let's now find a solution that suits us both".

Here are the steps to negotiate:

1.Define the conflict clearly

2.Propose solutions or alternatives together

3.Analyze the pros and cons of each proposed solution

4.Choose the one that has more advantages for both

5.Commit to implement it

6.Verify results

Conclusions

As we have seen, the basis for healthy self-esteem, an antidote against addictions, is built in childhood. Important then becomes the information to give to parents even before the child is born. Prevention is always better than cure.

If some reader should recognize himself as a teenager or adult in these two modes (dominant and / or dominated), do not hesitate to ask for help. Contrary to what you think, in fact, it is an act of "normality", because only those who have courage and awareness of their limits can try to overcome them, to live more serenely his life and his emotional relationships.

In addition to childhood experiences lived in the family or at school, can then aggravate the picture subsequent traumatic events, which may lead to suicide (if victims), murder (if executioners) or murder/suicide, as evidenced by many news stories.

If friends or family close to one or the other understand these issues, they are advised to take prompt action before the serious event occurs.

CPSIA information can be obtained
at www.ICGtesting.com
Printed in the USA
BVHW041346190121
598138BV00006B/120